Foundation

MATHEMATICS
GCSE for AQA
Problem-solving Book

Tabitha Steel, Coral Thomas, Mark Dawes and Steven Watson

CAMBRIDGE
UNIVERSITY PRESS

University Printing House, Cambridge CB2 8BS, United Kingdom

Cambridge University Press is part of the University of Cambridge.

It furthers the University's mission by disseminating knowledge in the pursuit of education, learning and research at the highest international levels of excellence.

www.cambridge.org
Information on this title:
www.cambridge.org/ukschools/9781107450103 (Paperback)

First published 2015

Printed in the United Kingdom by Latimer Trend

A catalogue record for this publication is available from the British Library

ISBN 978-1-107-45010-3 Paperback

Additional resources for this publication at www.cambridge.org/ukschools

Cover image © 2013 Fabian Oefner www.fabianoefner.com

Cambridge University Press has no responsibility for the persistence or accuracy of URLs for external or third-party internet websites referred to in this publication, and does not guarantee that any content on such websites is, or will remain, accurate or appropriate.

....

Contents

Introduction

What is a mathematical problem?

In everyday speech you might talk about a 'problem' as being something that is negative and often annoying. It might also be referred to as a difficulty, or as something that needs to be fixed.

Mathematical problems might be difficult, they might even be annoying, but they are certainly not negative! Some people see mathematical problems as any sort of mathematical question and some people use 'problem' in this way. For some people, 2 + 3 is just an easy question. 117 × 495 is more difficult but it is still just a question (even though some people will not know how to work it out).

The definition of a mathematical problem that this books uses is: something you don't know how to solve immediately.

117 × 495 could be worked out by writing down the number 117, adding on 117, and adding on another 117 again and again until you have written it 495 times. Even if you don't have a quicker way of working this out (and it would be a good idea to have a quicker way!) then this is not actually mathematical problem solving.

You often need to think 'around' a problem before you can get started.

A mathematical problem, then, is likely to be challenging, and it might well be the case that you can't 'see' the answer quickly. There are lots of things that might help you though, and this book will show you some of those ideas.

Different types of mathematics

To be able to do maths you need to know and understand mathematical ideas. These are important, and Cambridge University Press's *GCSE Mathematics for AQA Foundation Student Book* covers this sort of material. You also need to be able to solve problems, and this can be more difficult.

Problem-solving 'muscle memory'

When you learn to do something new you usually have to think very hard about what you are doing. For example, when someone first learns to drive a car they have to concentrate hard and decide which foot to press down, which way to move the gear stick, which mirror to look in, and so on.

Experienced motorists still need to concentrate on the road, but they don't need to think about the mechanics of every single action they take. This is known as 'muscle memory'. Muscle memory comes up lots in sports, so a footballer might have to train hard to learn how to do a rainbow flick, but will later be able to do it without thinking about it.

When you solve an equation the answer itself is often not very exciting ("$x = 3$ – big deal!"). The important thing when solving lots of equations is not finding out whether x happens to be 3 or 4 this time around, but that you are putting equation-solving in your muscle memory. Some of the problems you solve in this book *will* be interesting in their own right. We hope you will enjoy the challenge of doing them and will enjoy the answers too. Beyond this, though, you should not just work out the answers and be satisfied with that. After each problem, try to reflect on how you solved it. It is important to think about this, because this is the point at which you will learn new skills and this is how the muscle memory will start to develop.

Impossible to obvious

At first, a mathematical problem may appear to be impossible. When you know the answer or when you know how to do it, the problem can then seem obvious and not worth thinking about.

Hopefully you will avoid both of these extremes. None of the problems you will be asked to solve in this book are impossible – see them as a challenge. Even if a problem is obvious to you then there are still likely to be important ideas that you might be able to apply to other, more challenging problems in the future.

> A song by the band *Busted* has the chorus lyric: 'I've been to the year 3000, … and your great, great, great-granddaughter is pretty fine.'
>
> You might know the song (*Year 3000*) and might be concerned about the number of times 'great' is in the lyrics. First of all, how do we know we need more 'great's?
>
> Secondly, how many 'great's should there be?
>
> - Start working on this problem by yourself.
> - Talk to other people about what you have done.

How to use this book

Each chapter in this book covers a problem-solving strategy – a way of approaching a problem. The chapter starts by describing the strategy and how to apply it to a problem. This is followed by a number of questions that you can practise applying the strategy to.

Each question covers one or more strands of maths, which is shown by the colour wheel beside the question number.

 The exploded piece(s) of the colour wheel tells you what strand(s) of maths each question covers:

Number

Algebra

Ratio, proportion and rates of change

Geometry and measures

Probability

Statistics

The questions have been written to give you regular practice at problem solving so that you can build your skills, confidence and mathematical experience not only for your GCSE exams but also for life outside the classroom.

The star rating suggests the amount of problem-solving experience needed to tackle each question.

1 star questions are 'entry-level', they are good questions to start with.

2 star questions are ideal to move on to when you have confidently and successfully completed some of the entry-level questions.

3 star questions are for when you need more of a challenge.

In other words, the more stars there are, the more difficult the question is.

This means that you might need a calculator to work through the problem.

This means that you should work through a question without a calculator. If this is not present, you can use a calculator if you need to.

Tip

Tip boxes provide hints to help you work through questions.

Worked solutions to all of the questions are provided in the back of the book. Blue boxes alongside the solutions guide you through the working.

There is an old saying: 'A picture is worth a thousand words'.

So, if a diagram is not provided then draw one. It might be helpful, and could give you some ideas about how to solve the problem.

Draw a decent diagram. A sketch is probably fine, but it needs to look like the thing it describes. If there is a triangle in the problem, then your shape should be a triangle. If there is supposed to be a straight line then your line should be straight. The actual sizes of sides and angles are probably not important. Try to make your diagrams large and clear.

Label your diagram. If there is information provided in the question (such as the lengths of sides, or the sizes of angles) then write these on your diagram. This will often help when you are solving a problem.

Add new information that you work out. When you work out something new, add this to the diagram too.

So, in summary:

- draw a decent diagram
- annotate it
- add new information that you work out.

Here is a problem:

> A farmer has 22 fence panels and wants to use them to make a rectangular enclosure for his sheep. How many different enclosures can he make?

A picture of a field with sheep and lambs in it will not be helpful here.

Instead, a diagram of a rectangle would be more useful.

Now you can finish off this question.

The length and width of the rectangle add up to 11 (because the perimeter is 22 panels).

The dimensions that are possible are:

1 by 10	3 by 8	5 by 6
2 by 9	4 by 7	

So he can make 5 different enclosures.

It is fairly obvious what to do when a diagram has been provided as part of a question, but a diagram can sometimes be useful in other situations. Here is another example where drawing diagrams could help you.

At a fast food restaurant there is a 'meal deal' that involves first choosing one of the following: cheese burger, chicken burger, veggie burger or salad, and then ordering a side from the following list: fries, baked potato or coleslaw.

How many different meals could you have?

You could work systematically and create a list, but a diagram would also help.

The diagram above shows all the options and the lines show some of the possible combinations.

There are three lines coming from cheese burger. How many lines will come from chicken burger when the diagram is finished? Will this help you answer the question?

Alternatively, you could create a table like the one below to help you. What does each cell in this table represent? How does this table tell you, at a glance, how many meal possibilities there are?

	Fries	Baked potato	Coleslaw
Cheese burger			
Chicken burger			
Veggie burger			
Salad			

Each cell in the table is a possible meal deal combination. There are 12 cells in the table, therefore there are 12 different meals that you could have.

The following problems may be solved using more than one method; however, the worked solutions provided at the back of this book are based on the method introduced above.

Peter the factory manager planned to install a new hot drinks machine for the factory workers. He decided to fill it with tea as he thought tea was the most popular hot drink among the workers.

The workers did a survey to check what the preferred hot drink was among them. Each person surveyed could choose one drink from hot chocolate, tea and coffee.

Eight women wanted hot chocolate.

A total of 16 workers wanted tea, of which 7 were men.

10 men and 12 women chose coffee.

There were 25 men in total.

Was Peter correct?

Tip

What type of diagram would be useful here?

Here are the mock exam results (out of 100) in GCSE Mathematics and GCSE Statistics for a group of students (represented by letters A–L) .

	A	B	C	D	E	F	G	H	I	J	K	L
Mathematics	68	62	50	54	86	65	74	60	54	39	48	
Statistics	73	68	54	62	87	71	32	65	59	57	53	70

Tip

What type of diagram could you draw to help you see the link between the Maths and Statistics results?

Student L sat the GCSE Statistics examination and achieved a score of 70 but was ill during the GCSE Mathematics examination and could not complete the paper.

a Predict the Mathematics result for Student L.

b How good is your prediction likely to be?

c What is the statistical term for student G?

 A rectangle has length $(2x + 3)$ cm and width $(x - 1)$ cm.

The perimeter of the rectangle is 70 cm.

a Write an expression for the perimeter of the rectangle.

b How long is the longest side?

c Work out the area of the rectangle.

Ajit is making a lampshade, based on the design shown.

The lampshade consists of three cylinders covered in fabric.

How much fabric will Ajit need to make this lampshade?

Tip

You need to calculate the surface area of each cylinder in the lampshade. Remember that each cylinder is covered with a rectangle of fabric.

How much fabric is required to construct a tent like the one shown below?

The top vertex is above the middle of the square base.

Tip

What shapes do you need? Draw them and label them.

Margaret's garden contains lavender bushes and geraniums.

There is a row of six lavender bushes, then a row of ten geraniums, then six lavenders, then ten geraniums, and so on.

The rows alternate and finish with a row of lavender.

There are 70 geranium plants.

How many lavender bushes are there?

Two cafés record what types of drink they sell during a morning.

Type of drink	Frequency	
	Café A	Café B
Tea	28	15
Americano	22	8
Espresso	9	6
Latté	6	35
Cappuccino	7	26

a Write a list of all of the types of statistical graph you know how to draw.

b For each one say whether the graph is an appropriate way to represent this data.

c Draw the graph you think is most appropriate and say what it tells you.

Granny Bessie is making a patchwork quilt with scraps of fabric.

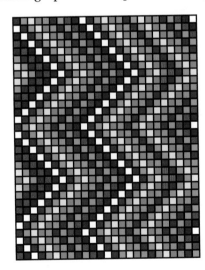

> **Tip**
>
> The diagram in the question is very detailed. Could a simpler diagram help?

Each patch is $(2x - 3)$ cm long and $(x + 3)$ cm wide.

a There are 25 patches in each row. Write a possible expression for the width of the quilt.

b There are 32 patches in each column. Write a possible expression for the length of the quilt.

The width of each patch is 8 cm.

c Calculate the dimensions of the quilt. Give your answer in metres.

In the local cement factory, the cement bags are placed on pallets made of planks of wood and bricks as shown in the diagram below.

The number of bricks needed to make the pallet is calculated as 'one more than the length of the plank in metres'.

a What length of pallet uses five bricks?

b If a pallet is 3 m long, how many bricks are used in it?

The factory needs pallets with a total length of 15 m for the next batch of cement it makes. It has planks of wood that are 4 m long and 3 m long.

c What combinations of planks can they have?

d How many bricks would be needed for each combination?

Sophie has a sheet of coloured paper and she wants to use it to cover a box.

The box is in the shape of a cuboid but it does not have a lid.

The dimensions of the base of the box are 20 cm by 10 cm and it has a height of 8 cm.

a What is the surface area of the exterior five faces of the box?

The walls of the box are 5 mm thick. To secure the paper and make it much neater Sophie would like to cover the inside of the box as well, but not the inside of the base.

Her sheet of paper measures 45 cm by 55 cm.

b Is the sheet of paper big enough for Sophie to cover the outside and inside walls of her box?

Geoff and Ravinder often have badminton and squash matches. The probability of Geoff winning at badminton is 0.85 and the probability of Geoff winning at squash is 0.35.

a What is the probability that the next time they play both matches, Geoff wins both?

b What is the probability that Geoff loses at badminton but wins at squash?

c What is the probability that both Geoff and Ravinder win one match each?

The probability Leela catches the 6:30 am train to Brighton is 0.7. If she misses the train she will be late for work.

The probability the train will be late is 0.15. If the train is late she will be late for work.

What is the probability Leela will be on time for work on a particular day?

Tip

What type of diagram might help?

In a cycling race, hill climbs are rated according to a category system. A category 5 climb is the easiest: it has an average slope of 3 : 100 (for every 100 m horizontal distance you climb 3 m vertically).

a What is the angle of the slope in a category 5 climb?

The hardest category of climb has an average slope of 1 : 10.

b How much steeper in degrees is this climb compared to the category 5 climb?

Jane left home at 9:30 am and walked at a speed of 5 kilometres per hour through the park until she reached the swings, which are 1250 metres from her house.

In the park she stopped to swing for 30 minutes.

After this, Jane continued for 1500 metres to Julie's house. She arrived there at 11:30 am.

Jane stayed at Julie's house until 3:00 pm. She then walked directly home, arriving at 4:40 pm.

a Copy and complete the travel graph for Jane's journey to and from Julie's house.

b At what speed did Jane walk for the second stage of her journey to Julie's house?

c What was Jane's average speed on her return journey in the afternoon?

Marianne needs to make a long-distance journey. She is looking for the cheapest possible car hire.
Whacky Wheels has a standard charge of £35, then 15p for every kilometre driven.
Wheelies Rentals has a charge of 23p per kilometre travelled.

a Draw the charges graph for both car hire companies.

Tip

In this question you can use the axes that are given to help you draw the diagram.

b Marianne thinks the return journey is 300 km.
Which company would be cheaper to use?

c Unfortunately, Marianne had made a mistake and the return
journey was 500 km.
How much money would Marianne have saved by using the other
hire company?

 16

The vertices of a quadrilateral are A, B, C and D.

A has coordinates (2, 1).

$$\overrightarrow{AB} = \begin{pmatrix} 2 \\ 3 \end{pmatrix}, \quad \overrightarrow{BC} = \begin{pmatrix} 4 \\ 0 \end{pmatrix}, \quad \overrightarrow{AD} = \begin{pmatrix} 4 \\ 0 \end{pmatrix}$$

a Write a column vector for $\overrightarrow{CD}$.

b Compare $\overrightarrow{CD}$ with $\overrightarrow{AB}$. What do you notice? Can you say why?

c What type of quadrilateral is ABCD?

Tip

Draw the shape on squared paper.

 17

Ann-Marie wants to plant a cherry tree in her garden.

She knows that when it is fully grown it will have a diameter of 3 m.

Ann-Marie wants all of the fruit to fall on her lawn.

Here is a sketch, not drawn to scale, of Ann-Marie's garden.

Tip

This diagram isn't drawn to scale
but your diagram should be.

Where could the tree be planted?

The diagram represents two remote towns labelled A and B in the Scottish Highlands.

Diagram not to scale

A

40 km

B

The mountain rescue helicopters from both towns will rescue any casualty within a radius of 25 km of town A or town B.
The fire brigade from town B will travel to any accident scene closer to town B than town A.

Draw a diagram and shade the region that the helicopter and fire brigade will both cover.

A projector is placed 1 m from a screen.
When the projector is turned on, the image produced on the screen is only 20 cm high.

How far back should the projector be moved in order to produce an image that fills the screen, which is approximately 1.5 m in height? (Assume that no other adjustments are made to the projector.)

a Harriet has a challenge for her classmate, Janet. "I'm thinking of a triangle", says Harriet:

- It has a right angle.

- It has one angle of 40°.

- It has one side that has a length of 5 cm.

"Can you draw my triangle, Janet?"

i Accurately construct a triangle that satisfies Harriet's conditions.

ii Demonstrate that there is more than one triangle that Harriet could be thinking of.

iii How could Harriet alter her challenge so that only one triangle is possible?

Tip

To construct an accurate triangle you may need to use a ruler, protractor and a pair of compasses.

Tip

Before you start your accurate construction, make some sketches to show the positions of the sides and angles you are given.

b Janet then comes up with a challenge for Harriet: "I'm thinking of a triangle":

- It has one side of length 4 cm.
- It has another side of length 7 cm.
- The angle in between these two sides is 55°.

"Can you draw my triangle, Harriet?"

i How many triangles satisfy Janet's conditions? Give reasons for your answer.

ii Measure the length of the third side.

 21 ✪✪✪

The probability of it raining on Tuesday is 0.15.
If it rains on Tuesday, the probability of it raining on Wednesday is 0.25.
If it does not rain on Tuesday, the probability of it raining on Wednesday is 0.45.

a Draw a tree diagram to show the possible outcomes.

b What is the probability it rains on both Tuesday and Wednesday?

c What is the probability it rains on only one of the days?

 22 ✪✪✪

The owner of a new bookshop carried out a survey to find the most popular A-level courses.
A total of 200 students were asked if they were studying Chemistry, Physics or Maths.

43 of the students surveyed did not study any of these three subjects.

A total of 92 were studying Chemistry.

There were 23 students studying both Chemistry and Maths, but not Physics.

There were 19 students studying both Physics and Maths, but not Chemistry.

29 students were studying only Physics, and there were a total of 74 students who studied Physics.

53 students were studying two of these three subjects.

a Display the information in a Venn diagram.

b If one person was chosen at random, what is the probability that they studied only Maths?

c If one person was chosen at random, what is the probability that they studied at least two of the subjects?

Caroline and Janet swim a total of 45 lengths each. They start together and finish together.

Caroline and Janet swim at different speeds for different swimming strokes but take 30 minutes to finish their 45 lengths.

Caroline swims 45 lengths of breaststroke, completing each one at the same speed.

Janet swims 20 lengths of front crawl in the first 10 minutes, then the remaining 25 lengths in the rest of the time.

a Is there a time when Caroline has swum more lengths than Janet?

b How long does it take Caroline to swim 30 lengths?

c What is Caroline's speed, in lengths per minute?

You can use the three transformations listed below.

A Reflect in the line $y = x$.

B Translate by vector $\begin{pmatrix} 1 \\ 0 \end{pmatrix}$.

C Enlarge by scale factor $\frac{1}{2}$ about the point (2, 3).

a Carry out all three transformations, in order, on a starting shape of your choice.

b How does the resulting image change if the transformations are applied in reverse order C → B → A?

Tip

You will find this question easier if you actually try it out.
Think about how you can make the question simpler by choosing particular shapes and certain side lengths that make the enlargement easier.

With some problems, it is easier not to focus straight away on the answer you need. Sometimes it is easier to work out want you **can** do and this might lead you to the answer you **need** almost by accident! Here is an example to demonstrate.

In this diagram, a square and an isosceles triangle sit on a straight line. Work out the size of angle A.

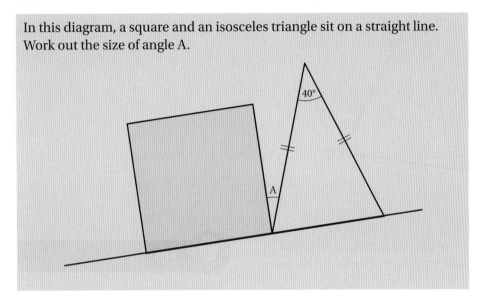

At the moment you can't work out angle A. But there are some things you **do** know.

There is a square in the diagram, so you can put in some angles.

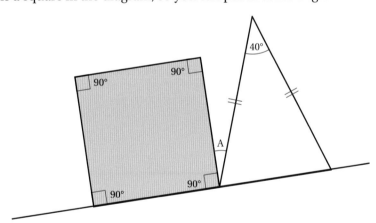

Some of these might not be helpful but, as there are only a few angles on the diagram, you are already narrowing down the problem.

Another piece of information you have got is that the triangle is isosceles. That means you can work out the other angles in the triangle. One angle is given as 40° and you know that all the angles in the triangle add up to 180°. This means the other two add up to 140° and because they are both equal they must each be 70°.

Now mark those angles on the diagram.

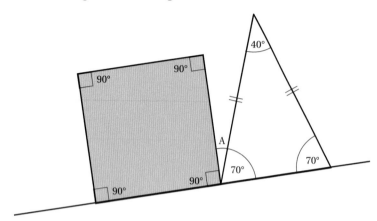

Now you can see what to do!

In the middle of the diagram there are three angles on a straight line. You know that these add up to 180° and you know what two of them are, so you can work out what angle A is.

$90° + 70° = 160°$

$180° - 160° = 20°$

So angle A = 20°

Now go back to the question.

In this diagram a square and an isosceles triangle sit on a straight line. Work out the size of angle A.

Check whether you missed out any important information. In this case, you will see that you have used all of the information provided in the question.

In this diagram a square (*you used the fact that angles in a square are 90°*) **and an isosceles triangle** (*you used the facts that base angles in an isosceles triangle are equal and that angles in a triangle add up to 180°*) **sit on a straight line** (*you used the fact that angles on a straight line add up to 180°*). **Work out the size of angle A.** (*You've done that.*)

The key points are: draw a good diagram, work out the things you can, and then write this new information on the diagram.

The following problems may be solved using more than one method; however, the worked solutions provided at the back of this book are based on the method introduced above.

Tip

Remember, angles on a straight line add up to 180°.

1

Without using a calculator, decide if the statement below is true or false.

$10\sqrt{64} < 80$

Give reasons for your answer.

2

The mean of five numbers is 12.

The numbers are in the ratio: $1:1:3:4:6$.

Find the largest number.

3

Jenny makes a kite. She starts from a square piece of paper, like this.

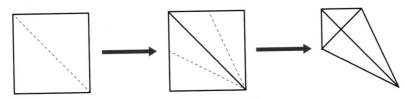

Jenny makes more kites and puts them together around a point.

The start of this pattern is shown in the diagram.

How many kites does she need altogether so they fit together without any gaps?

4

Andy decides to make a border for his garden using railway sleepers. He knows the length he needs is 20 metres.

When he gets to the garden centre he discovers each sleeper is $8\frac{1}{2}$ feet long and costs £22.

He knows that 1 foot is about 30 cm.

How much will it cost him to buy enough sleepers?

Karol is completely redecorating his living room. He needs to buy skirting board to put at the bottom of every wall.

Karol's living room is rectangular with two doorways, each of width 85 cm.

Skirting board costs £4.31 for a metre.

How much will it cost Karol to buy enough skirting board for his living room?

Tip

In this question some measurements are in metres and others are in centimetres.

Mrs Jones and Miss Smith are writing topic tests for GCSE Mathematics.

Each topic test will have 32 questions split in the ratio of 3 : 5 for non-calculator to calculator questions.

a How many non-calculator questions will each topic test contain?

There will eventually be 15 topic tests.

b How many calculator questions in total must be written?

Miss Smith is writing all of the non-calculator questions and some of the calculator questions so that she and Mrs Jones are each writing the same number of questions.

c What fraction of the total questions written by Miss Smith will be calculator questions?

Jo creates a quadrilateral by folding a rectangular piece of paper as shown in the diagram below.

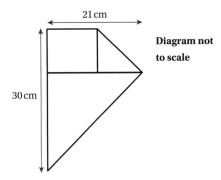

21 cm

30 cm

Diagram not to scale

a What is the area of the quadrilateral?

b What fraction of the original rectangle does the quadrilateral represent?

Tip

For part **b** you could give your answer as a fraction, decimal or percentage. If you choose to use a fraction, make sure you give it in its simplest form.

Lola draws some shapes on square dotted paper.

Which shape is the odd one out?

Tip

You might like to start thinking about the properties of each shape on its own.
You don't know which properties will be important so start with straightforward things like angles, sides, symmetry and area.

a Find a formula in terms of *x* for the area of the shape shown below.

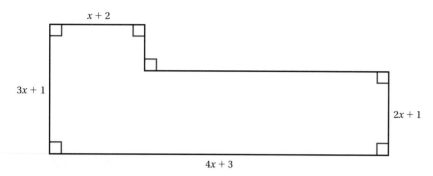

The actual length of the side labelled $3x + 1$ is 16 m.

b Solve the equation $3x + 1 = 16$.

c What is the area of the shape?

The shape is the plan of a field. Farmer Smith wants to put a fence around the field.

He plans to put three lengths of wire between wooden posts around the field, as shown in the diagram.

Farmer Smith will position the wooden posts one metre apart.

d How many wooden posts will Farmer Smith need in total?

e What total length of wire will he need?

Posts cost £18.50 each and wire is sold at £2.30 per metre.

f How much is it going to cost Farmer Smith to fence the field?

The teacher has a dice but doesn't know whether it is biased or not. 20 children each throw the dice 10 times.

The number of times each child rolls a six is shown below.

Is the dice biased? Give reasons for your ideas.

Child	A	B	C	D	E	F	G	H	I	J
Number of sixes in 10 rolls	7	4	3	6	4	3	4	5	5	3
Child	K	L	M	N	O	P	Q	R	S	T
Number of sixes in 10 rolls	4	5	6	4	5	7	0	3	3	2

A space probe took approximately ten years to reach Comet 67P, which is roughly three hundred million miles from Earth.

One of the fastest speeds recorded in a car was 290 miles per hour.

How many times faster was the space probe travelling?

Jeff takes a full 500 ml bottle of water and pours himself a drink into the glass shown on the right.

He fills the glass to 2 cm below the top.

How much water is left in the bottle?

Diagram not to scale

13 cm

6 cm

The height of the water in a cylindrical tube was 12 cm.

When two identical steel cubes were dropped into the tube the water level rose.

The diameter of the cylindrical tube is 8 cm.

The cubes are of side length 4 cm.

Calculate the increase in the height of the water.

Tip

The volume of a cylinder is $\pi r^2 h$.

Sandra wants to make a triangular prism:

She draws the diagram below, cuts it out, folds it up and tapes it together.

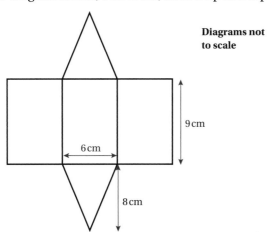

Diagrams not to scale

9 cm

6 cm

8 cm

a What is the volume of the triangular prism?

Chris makes a different prism:

The pentagonal faces each have an area of 36 cm².

The volume of Chris's prism is the same as the volume of Sandra's prism.

b Calculate the length of this prism.

length

Daniel is celebrating his thirteenth birthday by taking six friends paintballing.

He knows it costs £4.20 per person to hire the equipment and that they will also want to buy snacks and drinks.

Daniel's grandmother has given him £20 towards the cost of the trip and his friends will pay for the rest between them.

a   Write an inequality to model this situation.

b   What is the minimum amount of money that each of Daniel's friends must bring to cover the cost of the trip?

Tip

How much will the equipment cost to hire altogether?
How much money does Daniel have?

Rectangle A is 2 cm long and 3 cm high.

Rectangle B has an area of 12 cm².

Rectangle C has a perimeter of 20 cm.

Rectangle D has a length of 4 cm and an area of 24 cm².

Say which pair of rectangles must be mathematically similar.

 $\frac{4}{5}$ of the rectangle below is shaded.

40 units

30 units

a   How many extra unit squares must be shaded in order to increase this fraction to $\frac{5}{6}$?

The $\frac{4}{5}$-shaded rectangle is put next to a congruent rectangle that is $\frac{2}{3}$ shaded.

40 units

30 units

b   What fraction of the resulting large rectangle is shaded?

c   How many unit squares need to be shaded to increase the fraction so that exactly $\frac{3}{4}$ of the large rectangle is shaded?

Tip

Work out the area of the rectangle and then work out the shaded area. How does this help?

Alison is planning to make a patchwork quilt. She has chosen to include the flower pattern shown here as part of her design.

The centre piece of this pattern is a regular hexagon.

a Show that Alison cannot produce this pattern by using regular pentagons.

b She still wants to use a regular hexagon for the centre piece. Are there any regular polygons that she could put around the edge to form the petals?

c If she wanted to use regular pentagons for the petals, which regular polygon would she need in the centre?

Tip

What do you know about a regular hexagon? What angles can you work out? What about a regular pentagon?

Jamie goes to the local cake shop for the office tea break orders.

One day Jamie bought four cups of tea and six cupcakes. That order cost £9.20.

Another day, Jamie bought five cups of tea and two cupcakes. That came to a total of £7.10.

a Write an equation for Jamie's first visit to the shop.

b Write an equation for Jamie's second visit to the shop.

c Solve the equations and find the price of one cupcake and one cup of tea.

Tip

Let x represent the cost of a cup of tea and y represent the cost of a cupcake.

Javed's bike has a puncture.

He knows the circumference of his tyre is approximately 220 cm.

Replacement inner tubes are sized by diameter.

a What is the diameter of Javed's tyre?

A special device fixed to Javed's wheel measures the number of times the wheel turns and calculates the distance travelled.

b How far has Javed cycled when the device has measured 50 revolutions? Give your answer in metres.

c How many revolutions would the device record if Javed cycles the route shown in the diagram?

Give your answer to the nearest whole number.

Adding lines is a strategy that works for some geometry problems. Sometimes an extra line is very helpful. On other occasions it turns out to be useless. How can you tell which type of line to use? Let's work through an example problem.

In the diagram below, two parallel lines are shown. Work out the size of angle *a*.

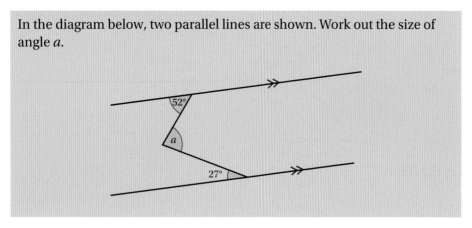

There are several different ways to solve this problem. Here are three of them, all of which involve adding extra lines to the diagram.

Solution 1

Add a line that is parallel to the other two lines and that passes through the angle you want to work out:

Could this help you?

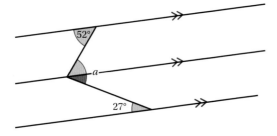

The angle shown in red is equal to 27°. Can you give reasons why?

What is the other part of angle α equal to? What is angle *a*?

Solution 2

Add a line that is perpendicular to the parallel lines and that passes through the point of the angle, as shown in the next diagram.

You now have two triangles. In those triangles you know two of the angles, so you can work out the third one. Do that now, remembering to mark the angles on the diagram. Here you are making use of the strategy from Chapter 2 and advice from Chapter 1 to annotate a diagram by adding new information to it when you work it out.

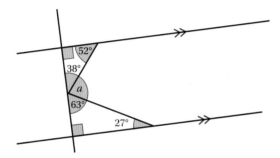

In the middle of this diagram there is a straight line, so now you can work out the missing angle *a*.

Solution 3

Add a line that is perpendicular to the parallel lines and that passes through the point of the 27° angle as shown in the diagram here.

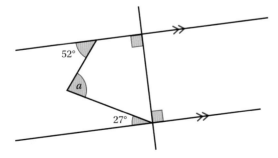

You can see a quadrilateral in the middle of the diagram. You can also 'see' what to do to solve the problem, because you can work out three of the angles in the quadrilateral and you know that all of the angles add up to 360°.

Go back to the question posed at the beginning: **How can you tell which type of line to use?**

The short answer is that you can't. There are lots of different lines you could have drawn on this diagram that wouldn't have helped you. For example, this line in the next diagram doesn't do anything special and is not helpful.

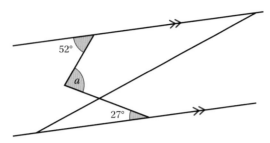

A line that is 'special' in some way is more likely to be helpful.

Try using lines that:

- are parallel to other lines
- are perpendicular to other lines
- are lines of symmetry
- join up two points
- are midpoints of sides of shapes.

Here is another example where extra lines make the question easier to answer.

The perimeter of this shape is 34.

Work out x.

You could work out the lengths of the other sides, but instead you could put two extra lines on the diagram.

Can you see why the perimeter of the rectangle is the same as the perimeter of the original shape?

The perimeter is $x + 10 + x + 10$, which equals 34.

This means $x = 7$.

The following problems may be solved using more than one method; however, the worked solutions provided at the back of this book are based on the method introduced above.

> **Tip**
>
> You might need to try out several ideas before one works!

An ant walks from vertex A to vertex G, always moving along the **edges** of the cuboid.

a   What distance does the ant walk if it goes from A to D to H to G?

b   What distance does the ant walk if it goes from A to G via vertex E, the hidden vertex of the cuboid?

c   Walking only on the edges, what is the shortest distance the ant could walk if it started at vertex B and returned to vertex B without walking on any edge twice?

d   Investigate the longest distance the ant could walk if it went from vertex B to vertex H and back to vertex B, but without travelling the same edge more than once.

Liz looks up at the clock on her wall. She is disappointed to see that it is not yet 5 pm, which is the time she can go home.

a   Through how many degrees must the minute hand of the clock turn before Liz can leave work?

b   Through what angle must the hour hand turn before Liz can leave work?

 Tip

Remember that, on an analogue clock, the hour hand moves continuously, just like the minute hand. What angle does each hand turn through in one hour?

3

ABCD is a rectangle. $\overrightarrow{AB}$ is **a** and $\overrightarrow{BC}$ is **b**.

Is $\overrightarrow{AC}$ the same as $\overrightarrow{DB}$? Give reasons for your answer.

4 ⭐⭐☆

Gerry has a swimming pool at his holiday home. He wants to put a short fence around the pool, to prevent small children falling in.

Diagram not to scale

Pool

15 m

> **Tip**
>
> Draw good diagrams!

He wants the fence to surround the pool, shown in the diagram, completely and at a distance of 1 m from its edge.

a Calculate the length of fencing that Gerry will need to buy. Give your answer correct to 3 significant figures (sf).

Ian needs to build a fence around his pool, but it is a different shape from Gerry's as shown in the next diagram.

Ian would like to build his fence at a distance of 1.5 m from the edge of his pool.

7 m

20 m

b Will Ian need to buy more fencing than Gerry? Give reasons for your answer.

5 ⭐⭐☆

Jimmy the window cleaner has a ladder made of three sections.

The first section is the longest, the second section is 60 cm shorter and the third section is 60 cm shorter than the second one.

The total length of the three sections is 5.1 m.

How long is each section of Jimmy's ladder?

Lorna is travelling from London to Glasgow and is choosing from two options for travel.

Lorna can go by coach, which travels direct from London to Glasgow. Alternatively, she can go by train to Glasgow with a change in Birmingham and a wait of 1 hour 45 minutes.

The distance from London Victoria to Glasgow Station is 650 km.

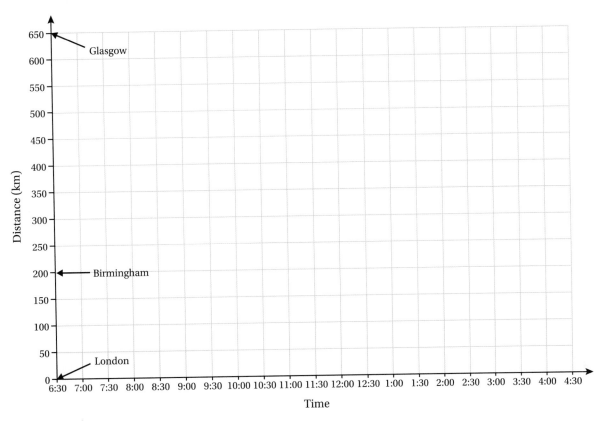

The coach leaves at 6:30 am and takes exactly 8 hours to arrive in Glasgow.

If Lorna goes by train she would leave Victoria station at 7 am and arrive in Birmingham station at 8:40 am.

The train journey from Birmingham to Glasgow should then take 4 hours and 15 minutes.

a What is the average speed for the coach journey?

b What is the average speed for the train journey?

Quadrilateral ABCD is drawn on this coordinate grid.

Quadrilateral EFGH is mathematically similar to ABCD.

Length AB corresponds to length EF as shown on the grid.

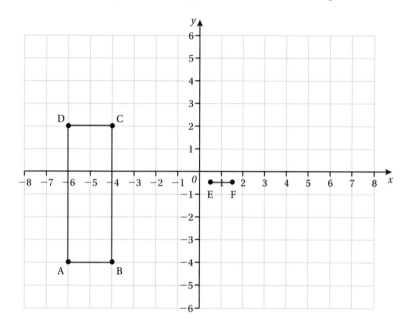

What are the coordinates of points G and H?

Show that the two right-angled triangles in the diagram below have the same area.

Tip

What can you work out in these triangles?

Show how the shape shown here could be divided up:

a to create **three** congruent shapes

b to create **four** congruent shapes.

Students taking part in a mathematical challenge are shown this diagram.

They are asked the question: **What proportion of the outer triangle is coloured purple?**

After some thought the teams hand in their answers. Four of these answers are shown below:

Team **A**: $24\,\text{cm}^2$

Team **B**: $\dfrac{3}{4}$

Team **C**: $\left(\dfrac{3}{4}\right)^2$

Team **D**: 0.5625

The question is marked out of 4 marks. How many marks would you award each each? Give reasons for your decisions.

Mandeep is investigating patterns in circles. He draws eight dots equally spaced around a circle.

He draws a triangle by connecting three of the dots. The line AC passes through the centre of the circle, O.

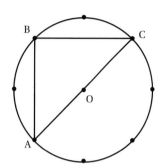

a Use this image to show that ∠ABC is a right angle.

He draws another triangle by connecting a different set of three dots. The line AC still passes through the centre of the circle.

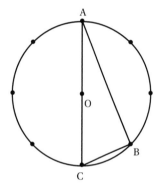

b Is ∠ABC still a right angle?

Mandeep draws a different circle and marks 10 dots equally spaced around its circumference.

Once again, he draws a triangle ABC by connecting three of these dots.

The line AC passes through the centre of the circle.

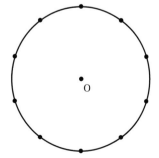

c Show that, for a triangle of your choice that meets these conditions, the sum of angle BAC and angle BCA is still 90°.

A pizza restaurant offers two styles of pizza: classic and rustic. The classic pizza is a standard circular pizza.

The rustic pizza is a different shape; it is rectangular with semi circular ends as shown in the diagram.

The restaurant charges more for the rustic pizza, but do you actually get more for your money?

7 inches

12 inches

18 inches

Rustic

Classic

Tip

Remember to justify your answer, using numbers and words. Your conclusions must be convincing.

ABCDEF is a regular hexagon.

A has coordinates (2, 1).

The column vector $\overrightarrow{AB} = \begin{pmatrix} 0 \\ 2 \end{pmatrix}$.

a What is the column vector for $\overrightarrow{DE}$?

The coordinates of C are $(2 + \sqrt{3}, 4)$.

b What is the column vector for $\overrightarrow{BC}$?

c What is the column vector for $\overrightarrow{FC}$?

d What is the column vector for $\overrightarrow{AE}$?

e What is the column vector for $\overrightarrow{AC}$?

f What is the column vector for $\overrightarrow{EF}$?

 14

Charlie's house has two floors connected by a staircase.

The vertical distance between the two floors is 3.6 m.

Each step in the staircase is 18 cm high and 28 cm deep.

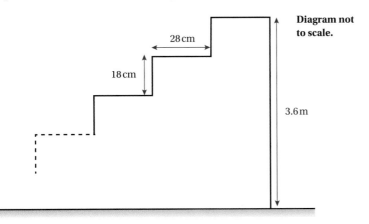

28 cm

18 cm

3.6 m

Diagram not to scale.

Tip

The diagram is a useful start but is missing some important lines.

a How many steps are there in the staircase?

b How long will the banister rail be?

31

✪✪✪

Children on a field trip are told that they can use a clever trick to estimate the height of a tall tree.

They are told to point their arm at an angle of approximately 45° and to look along it.

They then walk backwards until their arm is pointing to the top of the tree.

The distance from the child to the tree trunk is approximately the same as the height of the tree.

a Say why this method gives a rough answer.

Two children, Kelly and Guy, try this out. They are both the same height. Guy ends up standing 3 m in front of Kelly.

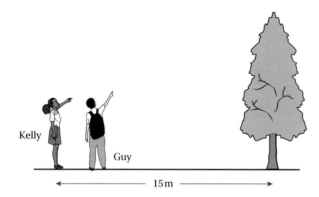

b If Kelly's angle is exactly 45°, at what angle must Guy (who is 3 m in front of her) be holding his arm?

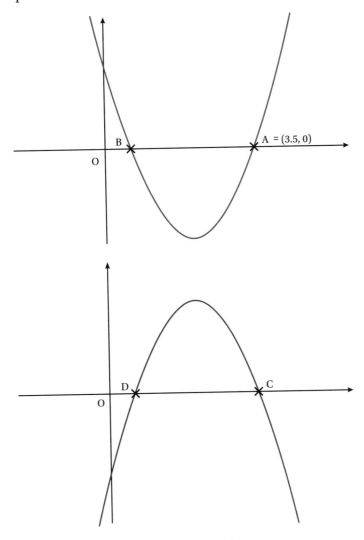

16

The graphs of two quadratic equations are shown below.

The blue parabola is symmetrical about the line $x = 2$ and has roots at A and B.

The blue parabola is reflected in the x-axis to create the red parabola. The red parabola has roots at C and D.

Work out the coordinates of points B, C and D.

Sometimes there is a problem that is just too complicated to solve immediately. One way to deal with this is to make the problem simpler. This won't directly tell you the answer because it will be a slightly different problem, but it might give you a starting point that will help you get to the answer. Here's an example.

George climbs a flight of 10 stairs. He can go from one stair to the next one (1-step), or can miss out a stair and go up two at once (2-step). How many different ways can he go up the 10 stairs?

You could start by drawing a diagram, but you will quickly produce a picture that has too many lines on it.

You could also start to write down the different possibilities, using 1 to stand for '1-step' and 2 to stand for '2-step'.

So:

1111111111

1211212

22222

and so on.

But there are too many possibilities and it just looks too hard.

You could make the problem simpler. Let's make it very simple indeed. Imagine that George wants to climb a flight of stairs that has 1 stair in it. This is easy: 1 way (if he tries to do a 2-step he will only actually go up one step). Now try a flight with 2 stairs in it. There are two ways. The diagram below shows the working.

Flight with 1 stair

1 way   1

Flight of 2 stairs

                               1   1

2 ways   2

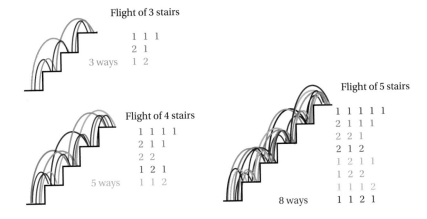

Flight of 3 stairs

1	1	1
2	1	
1	2	

3 ways

Flight of 4 stairs

1	1	1	1
2	1	1
2	2	
1	2	1
1	1	2

5 ways

Flight of 5 stairs

1 1 1 1 1
2 1 1 1
2 2 1
2 1 2
1 2 1 1
1 2 2
1 1 1 2
1 1 2 1

8 ways

You could now look at the pattern of answers to see if that will help, as shown in this table.

Do you recognise the number sequence in the second column?

1, 2, 3, 5, 8 is part of the Fibonacci Sequence, where you add the two previous numbers to get the next one. $1 + 2 = 3$, $2 + 3 = 5$, $3 + 5 = 8$. If this is the right sequence then the next one will be $5 + 8 = 13$. You don't want to draw this out, so instead think about why this might be sensible.

When you look at the numbers written next to each flight of stairs you can see some similarities.

Number of stairs	Number of ways of climbing them
1	1
2	2
3	3
4	5
5	8

Here are the routes up the 5-stair flight:

11111
2111
221
212
1211
122
1112
1121

If you remove the final number you get this sequence:

1111
211
22
21
121
12
111
112

← and these are the ways of climbing a 3-stair and a 4-stair flight!

Why does that make sense?

Well, if you want to climb a 5-stair flight of stairs, you could go up 4 stairs and then do a 1-step to get to the top. So you need all of the ways of climbing a 4-stair flight and can then put a 1 at the end. Alternatively, you can get to stair 3 and then do a 2-step to get to the top, so you need all of the ways of climbing a 3-stair flight with a 2 after them. This means you really are adding the previous two numbers together.

To climb a 10-stair flight you need to continue the sequence and get: 1, 2, 3, 5, 8, 13, 21, 34, 55, 89. So, there are 89 ways to climb the 10 stairs.

Here, simplifying the problem meant you could get started and could see what was going on.

Let's look at another example problem.

> What is the smallest number that can be divided (with no remainder) by all of the numbers from 1 to 12?

What do you know already?

Clearly the number will have to end with a zero (to make it divisible by 10). It will have to be even so it is divisible by 2 (but if it ends with a zero then that is already the case).

One strategy that might be useful is to make the problem simpler.

Change the problem so that it now says this:

What is the smallest number that can be divided by all of the numbers from 1 to 3?

If you do $2 \times 3 = 6$ then you know that can be divided by 1, by 2 and by 3. Is it the smallest number? Yes.

Another change:

What is the smallest number that can be divided by all of the numbers from 1 to 4?

If you do $2 \times 3 \times 4 = 24$ then you know that can be divided by 1, by 2, by 3 and by 4. But there is a smaller number that works. 12 can be divided by 1, by 2, by 3 and by 4. Why didn't $2 \times 3 \times 4$ give you the right answer? To make it divisible by 4 you didn't need to multiply the previous answer by 4, because there was already a 2 involved. If you had just multiplied that previous answer by 2 that would have given you something that is divisible by 4.

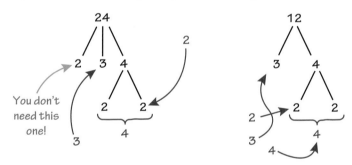

Therefore the answer is $2 \times 3 \times 2 = 12$

Do you notice that these numbers are prime numbers?

Try the next one:

What is the smallest number that can be divided by all of the numbers from 1 to 5?

You currently have $2 \times 3 \times 2$, which is not helpful if you want it to be divisible by 5. The trick that you used with 4 (splitting it into 2×2) won't work here because 5 is a prime number. To make it a multiple of 5 you will need to multiply by 5, giving you $2 \times 3 \times 2 \times 5 = 60$

You can see that the next one is easy.

What is the smallest number that can be divided by all of the numbers from 1 to 6?

60 is obviously already divisible by 6, and you can see that in the numbers because 2×3 is in there. $2 \times 3 \times 2 \times 5$ is divisible by all of the numbers from 1 to 6.

To make the smallest number divisible by 7 you need to include a 7, because you cannot make 7 by multiplying smaller numbers (7 is prime).

To make it divisible by 7 you therefore need to have $2 \times 3 \times 2 \times 5 \times 7$

To make it divisible by 8 you only need an extra 2 because it is already divisible by 4, and to make it divisible by 9 you need an extra 3.

You know it is already divisible by 10 (because it ends with a zero).

11 is a prime number so you need to have $2 \times 3 \times 2 \times 5 \times 7 \times 2 \times 3 \times 11$

The first three numbers in this product make 12 ($2 \times 3 \times 2$) so it is divisible by 12.

Your final answer is therefore: $2 \times 3 \times 2 \times 5 \times 7 \times 2 \times 3 \times 11 = 27\,720$

The following problems may be solved using more than one method; however, the worked solutions provided at the back of this book are based on the method introduced above.

> **Tip**
>
> There are other ways to solve this problem, such as realising that the question is really the same as asking for the lowest common multiple of the numbers 1 to 12.

 Simon and Jamie are playing a game of 'Guess the number'.

Jamie says, "If I multiply my number by 7 and then subtract 10, my final answer is 25."

a What was Jamie's number?

Simon takes his turn. "If I add 9 to my number then divide by 4, my final answer is 5."

b What was Simon's number?

> **Tip**
>
> Working backwards from the answers should lead to the starting value.

Farmer Jones is constructing pig runs for his prize pigs. He is making them hexagonal in shape.

The hexagons will be regular and each side will be made of three panels, each of exactly the same length.

Farmer Jones wants the pens each to have a perimeter of 10.8 m.

What will be the length, in metres, of each panel?

> **Tip**
>
> Write the equation which describes the perimeter of the pen.

Frances has 40 cubes to pack into a box.

Each cube has sides of length 5 cm.

a Sketch a box that will hold all the cubes without any spaces.

b Write the dimensions of the box on your diagram.

A cinema offers discounted tickets on Thursdays.

Normal tickets

Adult: £7.60   Child: £3.40

Thursday tickets

Adult: £7.00   Child: £2.95

The cinema has 150 seats.

Calculate the percentage difference in the amount the cinema gets on a Thursday compared to other days, in the following situations.

a The cinema is completely filled with adults.

b The cinema is completely filled with children.

c The cinema is filled with families (with the same number of adults and children).

Consider each of the calculations below.

Without using a calculator, decide whether the answer is odd or even and say why.

a $4^3 + 3^4 = ?$

b $6^7 + 3^7 = ?$

> **Tip**
>
> What type of number (odd or even) is 4^3?

Ahmed buys a piece of wood measuring 12 cm by 5 cm by 1 m for £5.

He uses the piece of wood to make 40 door wedges like the one in the diagram below.

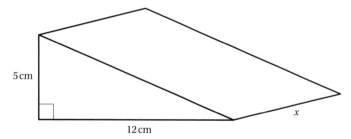

a What is the width, x, of the wedges?

b What is the lowest price Ahmed could sell the wedges for to make at least £30 profit?

Helen drives to work every day.

On her journey there is a level crossing, a set of traffic lights and a roundabout.

At each of these either she must stop or she is allowed to continue.

STOP when lights show

The probability of stopping at the level crossing is $\frac{1}{10}$.

The probability of stopping at the lights is $\frac{1}{4}$.

The probability of stopping at the roundabout is $\frac{2}{3}$.

What is the probability that on Helen's next journey to work she has to stop at least once?

 Tip

What happens if there is only the level crossing? Is there a diagram that would help with this? Then you could introduce the traffic lights too.

You want to hire a bouncy castle for a party.

Spring High has a basic charge of £18 plus £1.80 for every hour.

Castle Jump has a basic charge of £20 plus £1.30 per hour.

You might need the castle for up to 5 hours.

a Copy the axes shown below and plot a graph to show the charges for Spring High.

b Using your graph, find the price Spring High would charge you to have the bouncy castle from 6 pm until 11 pm.

c On the same axes, plot a graph for Castle Jump's charges.

d For what length of time would the charge be the same for both companies?

 Tip

To start your graphs, plot how much it would cost to have the bouncy castle for 0 hours.
Then work out how much it would cost for 1 hour.

Calculate the missing length on the trapezium.

Tip

Look for the right-angled triangle in the diagram.

Two almost identical logos are shown in the diagram below.

Both show a square of side length 10 cm with a second square tilted inside it.

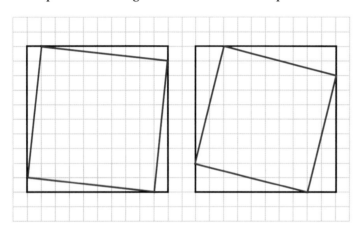

Do they have the same total line length?

Tip

How could you work out the lengths of one of the red lines?

Is it possible for you to count from one to a million in your lifetime?

Larry's aunt gives Larry £40 000 to put into a compound interest savings account.

ABC Bank is offering 8% compound interest on your money if you invest more than £30 000 and it remains in the bank for at least ten years.

Larry's aunt tells him that his money will more than double if he invests his money for ten years.

a Is Larry's aunt correct?

b How much will Larry have in his account at the end of ten years?

Larry's aunt decides to invest some of her own money for ten years. She wants to make a profit and have a total of at least £75 000 at the end of the ten-year period.

Tip

In order to answer this question you will need to make some estimations based on various assumptions. You should also round your answers to an appropriate degree of accuracy. You might like to consider how long it takes you to count from one to ten.

c What is the smallest amount (to the nearest £1000) Larry's aunt must invest to have at least £75 000 at the end of ten years?

 13

Anna knows that she can create a heart shape from a triangle and two semicircles. She makes a Valentine's card by cutting a heart shape out of a rectangle of red cardboard 9 cm by 13 cm, as shown below.

What area of red cardboard has Anna removed from the original piece to make her card? Give your answer correct to 3 sf.

Tip

Start simply. Find the radius of the circle first. Can you then find the areas you need?

 14

Dave makes the 280 km journey from Milton Keynes to Weymouth. Dave travels by car, and his travel graph is shown.

Hazel was travelling from Weymouth to Milton Keynes on the same day as Dave but Hazel rides a motorcycle.

Hazel's travel graph is also shown in the figure.

Both Dave and Hazel set out on their journeys at 9:00 am.

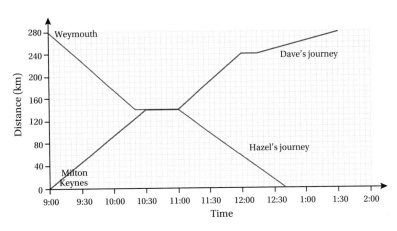

a What was Dave's speed for the first 140 km?

b What was Hazel's speed for the first stage of her journey?

c How long did Hazel have to wait before Dave arrived at the service station where they were meeting for a coffee?

d Dave got caught up in a queue following an accident with a tractor just outside of Weymouth. What time was this?

e How long did Dave's journey take? What was his average speed?

f How long did Hazel's journey take? What was her average speed?

In the UK the national speed limit on motorways is 70 miles per hour. To convert kilometres to miles, divide by 8 and multiply by 5.

g Should either of them receive a speeding ticket for any stage of their journeys?

Making changes to the problem is another strategy that works particularly well with some geometric problems. This time you won't necessarily simplify the problem (like you did in Chapter 4) but you could instead tweak it in a way that doesn't change the important features of the problem. This might allow you to see what is going on.

In this diagram AB is the diameter of the circle, C lies on the circumference and O is the centre of the circle.

What is the relationship between the area of triangle OAC and the area of triangle OBC? Give reasons for your answer.

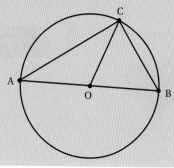

The question asks 'What is the relationship?' What could that mean? Perhaps one is double the other? Maybe they are the same?

In this diagram it looks as if the areas might be the same. Can you provide evidence to convince yourself that this is the case? Can you convince someone else?

The key points are

- there is a circle

- AB is the diameter of the circle

- O is the centre of the circle

- points A, B and C are on the circle.

All of this must stay true. You might be able to move some of the points so the answer is obvious. There doesn't seem to be anything special about the placing of point C, so it might be acceptable to move the points around. It wouldn't be acceptable to move C off the circle, though, because that would change the scenario.

This diagram looks good. C has moved so that it is halfway between A and B but still on the circle. There is now a line of symmetry in the diagram and the two triangles are clearly equal.

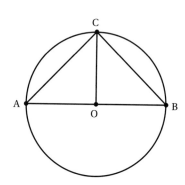

Here is another special case.

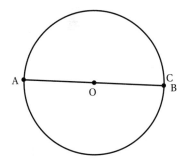

C has moved so that it is on top of point B. This time the two triangles both have zero area, so they are the same.

The idea that the two areas are the same is looking plausible.

How do you work out the area of a triangle?

It is half of the base multiplied by the perpendicular height.

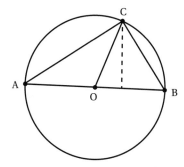

In the right-hand triangle, the area is the radius of the circle (OB) multiplied by the dotted line (the perpendicular height), divided by 2.

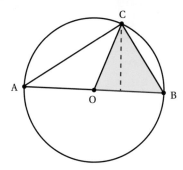

In the left-hand triangle, the area is the radius of the circle (AO) multiplied by the perpendicular height, divided by 2. But what is the perpendicular height for the left-hand triangle? It is actually the dotted line.

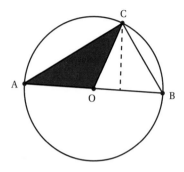

So they do have the same area and you can say why.

This is also an example of where adding an extra line can help us (see Chapter 3).

So, what sort of changes might be useful?

- Moving points around (but preserving the initial scenario).
- Trying to make a special situation (for example, a line of symmetry).
- Moving points to extreme positions.

A good diagram is also important here (see Chapter 1).

Here is another problem.

> Triangular numbers can be shown as stacks of squares like this:
>
> There are 10 squares, so 10 is a triangular number.
>
> The triangular numbers are 1, 3, 6, 10, 15, 21, 28, and so on.
>
> Show that if you add two adjacent triangular numbers you always get a square number.

You could try this out:

$1 + 3 = 4$ $3 + 6 = 9$ $15 + 21 = 36$

This looks good but how do you know it will always be true?

If you draw a square around a triangular number what happens?

The empty space looks interesting. Now push the squares over to the side:

The red part is a triangular number and the white part is the previous triangular number!

So you have shown that adding two adjacent triangular numbers always gives a square number.

The following problems may be solved using more than one method; however, the worked solutions provided at the back of this book are based on the method introduced above.

What is the **same** and what is **different** about the pairs of calculations below?

a $\frac{1}{3} + 1$ and $1 + \frac{1}{3}$

b $1 - \frac{1}{3}$ and $\frac{1}{3} - 1$

Three pairs of fractions are shown below. In each case the smaller fraction is on the left-hand side.

i $\frac{1}{4} < \frac{1}{2}$ **ii** $\frac{5}{8} < \frac{5}{7}$ **iii** $\frac{2}{6} < \frac{4}{10}$

How could you change one of the fractions in each pair so that the smaller fraction was on the right-hand side?

Describe the mathematical process that will change the fraction in each case.

> **Tip**
>
> Be specific about how you have changed a fraction.
> - Have you multiplied or divided it by something? If so, by what?
> - Have you added something? If so, what have you added?
> - Have you subtracted something? If so, what have you subtracted?

Alina is asked to write down five different fractions in ascending order.

She thinks carefully and then writes:

$$\frac{1}{6} \qquad \frac{1}{5} \qquad \frac{1}{4} \qquad \frac{1}{3} \qquad \frac{1}{2}$$

a Suggest another set of fractions that Alina could have written.

b Suggest another set of fractions where none has a numerator of 1.

c Suggest a final set of fractions all of which have their numerator greater than their denominator.

> **Tip**
>
> There are lots of ways to do this. One way is to change the original set of fractions.

$23.64 \times 805 = 1903.02$

How can you tell that this statement is incorrect?

> **Tip**
>
> How could you change the question to make it obvious that there is a mistake?

Felix bought some lily bulbs. The lilies will be white, purple or red in colour.

The probability of the first lily to flower being red is $\frac{1}{5}$. The probability of the first lily to flower being purple is 0.7.

a What is the probability that the first lily to flower will be white?

b If Felix bought 140 lily bulbs, how many of them will produce purple flowers?

Unfortunately $\frac{1}{7}$ of the 140 bulbs fail to grow.

c How many of the remaining bulbs would you expect to produce red flowers?

Which is bigger?

a 400 g + 400 mg   or   0.5 kg – 90 g

b 0.1 km + 150 cm   or   110 m – 900 cm

c 0.75 hours + 600 seconds   or   50 minutes + 0.1 hours

Tip

Remember that to compare quantities, they need to be measured in the same units.

This is the flag of the Seychelles (an island off the coast of Africa).

The top and the right-hand side are both divided into thirds.

Is the area of the white triangle bigger, smaller or the same as the area of the blue triangle? Give reasons for your answer.

Four snails have a race.

Tip

In order to compare the snails you will need to convert their speeds into the same units.

Assuming that the snails move at a constant speed to the finish line, which one will get there first?

9

I choose three consecutive integers and add them together. $5 + 6 + 7 = 18$

I notice that 18 is also the result of 6×3.

I select another set of three integers and add them together. $2 + 3 + 4 = 9$

I notice that 9 is also the result of 3×3.

It looks like the sum of three consecutive integers is the same as the middle integer multiplied by three.

a Is this always true?

b Can you find a rule for adding four consecutive integers?

c How might you extend your rule to add five or more consecutive integers?

10

Lois is moving house. She has 600 CDs.
Each CD case measures 142 mm × 125 mm × 10 mm.

a How many of her CDs can she pack into this box?

b How many more boxes will she need to be able to transport all of the CDs?

 Tip

A good diagram will help.

11

Daisy draws a shape on a coordinate grid as shown in the diagram below.

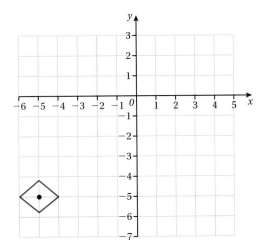

a Daisy notices that the centre of her shape (marked with the black dot on the diagram) lies on the line $x = -5$.

How could Daisy translate her shape so that its centre remains on the line $x = -5$?

b Daisy's shape also lies on the line $y = x$.

How could you translate Daisy's shape so that its centre remains on the line $y = x$?

 Tip

Remember to use vector notation to describe a particular translation.
Is there more than one solution to each part of this question? If so, can you write your answers in a more general way (using words or mathematical notation)?

47

Mikey is asked to investigate what happens when a shape is reflected in two perpendicular mirror lines in turn.

He draws the following picture and makes the observation, "Ah! It's just the same as a translation of the original shape."

Tip

'Perpendicular mirror lines' means that the mirror lines are at right angles (90°) to each other. Why did Mikey choose his pair of mirror lines to be the *x*- and *y*-axes? Are there other pairs that he could have chosen?

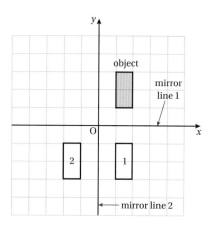

Mikey's teacher looks at his work and asks, "Are you sure?"

a Suggest what Mikey could do next in his investigation to find out.

b By considering the starting point shown in the diagram below, decide whether or not you agree with Mikey's first idea.

Melissa is starting a business. She has designed the logo shown below.

It is based on an isosceles triangle with a semicircle on each side.

Calculate the perimeter of Melissa's logo.

Tip

Remember, you can use Pythagoras' theorem to calculate unknown lengths in right-angled triangles.

When you have done a lot of problem solving you may find that you come across problems that are similar to others you have worked on in the past. Even if they are not identical you might find that some of the ideas you used in the earlier problem can help you out. Here is an example.

> Multiply two consecutive even numbers. Do you always get a multiple of 8? Give reasons for your answer.

You could start by trying a few out to see if it appears to be true (but this won't prove it if you think it is the case):

$2 \times 4 = 8$ $4 \times 6 = 24$

$6 \times 8 = 48$ $10 \times 12 = 120$

All of these are multiples of 8. It is looking good so far (but you haven't shown why).

How could you approach this problem? Think of maths topics that might be relevant. You could look at factors, but you could also use some algebra.

Try writing an algebraic expression for the problem. What can you use for the two numbers? If you call them a and b then that doesn't include the idea that they are **even** numbers. If you call them $2a$ and $2b$ then that could help. You need a and b to be consecutive whole numbers. This tells us that either a or b is even. If you do $2a \times 2b$ you get $4ab$ but one of a and b is even so the whole thing must be a multiple of 8.

Here is a slightly more formal way to do the same thing, using just a single letter. If the first even number is $2a$ then you can call the next one $2a + 2$. When you multiply these you get $2a(2a + 2)$. This is equal to $4a^2 + 4a$, which is $4a(a + 1)$.

Let's look at $4a(a + 1)$.

If a is odd then $a + 1$ is even and we have $4 \times$ odd $\times$ even, which is a multiple of 8 (because 4 multiplied by an even number is a multiple of 8). If $a + 1$ is odd then a is even and we have $4 \times$ even $\times$ odd, which is a multiple of 8. So the whole thing is a multiple of 8.

Here is another example.

> Choose any three consecutive positive integers. Add them together. Is the answer always a multiple of 3? Is the answer always a multiple of 6? Give reasons for your answer.

This problem is similar to the previous one, so you could use some similar techniques. First, try a few numbers just to get a feel for what is going on. Then use some algebra and try to create an expression to describe what is happening.

$1 + 2 + 3 = 6$ – this is a multiple of 3 and also a multiple of 6

$2 + 3 + 4 = 9$ – this is a multiple of 3 but is not a multiple of 6

You have already shown that the answer is **not** always a multiple of 6 because you have found one that doesn't work.

Using algebra, you could call the first number a. The next number will therefore be $a + 1$ and the one after that will be $a + 2$. This is similar to what we did in the previous example so you are using the experience you gained doing that question.

When you add these together you get $a + a + 1 + a + 2$, which equals $3a + 3$. To show that this is clearly divisible by 3 you could factorise: $3(a + 1)$, to show that you have an integer $(a + 1)$ multiplied by 3.

If you call the middle number n then it happens to be even easier. The three numbers are: $n - 1$, n, $n + 1$, and adding these gives $3n$. Note that you didn't use three different letters to describe the numbers. This is often useful.

The following problems may be solved using more than one method; however, the worked solutions provided at the back of this book are based on the method introduced above.

Two handprints are shown in the diagram below.

Approximately how many times bigger is handprint A than handprint B?

> **Tip**
>
> This is a question about area. The handprints have been shown on a square grid. How many different ways could you use this to estimate the area of each handprint? Which method is better for this particular question?

For each pair of decimal numbers below decide which is smaller. Say how you know in each case.

a 1.099 and 1.308

b 0.5 and 0.500

c 1.7 and 1.534

> **Tip**
>
> This is not really problem solving, but the difficult part here might be saying how you know.

3

The perimeter of this isosceles triangle is 41 cm.

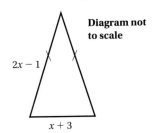

Diagram not to scale

$2x - 1$

$x + 3$

What are the lengths of the three sides?

Tip

Can you write the perimeter using algebra? What is this algebra equal to?

4

Razi has taken up golf and often goes to the golf range. He noticed that in every bucket of 30 balls he gets four yellow balls.

a Razi randomly picks a ball from the bucket. What is the probability that the first ball Razi uses is a yellow ball?

Razi stayed all morning and used five buckets of balls.

b How many of the balls he used were yellow?

c What is the probability that Razi's furthest shot that day was with a yellow ball? Simplify your answer.

5

Jeremy makes lemonade using 2.5 litres of water, 500 millilitres of concentrated sugar solution and 750 millilitres of lemon juice.

a Express these quantities as ratios.

b How many litres of lemonade does Jeremy make?

This lemonade is too sweet, so Jeremy makes another batch using half the amount of sugar solution but keeps the quantities of the other ingredients the same.

c Express Jeremy's quantities as a ratio.

d How much lemonade did Jeremy make with his new recipe?

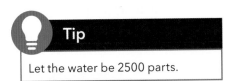

Tip

Let the water be 2500 parts.

A farmer has started making crisps to sell at the weekly farmers' market. She asks her husband and son to pack the crisps for her each week. They must make each packet a similar weight.

At certain times the farmer does a random test on some of the packets.

These were the results one day:

Husband: 57.8 g, 61.1 g, 62.3 g, 58.9 g, 59.5 g, 60.6 g, 60.1 g, 58.8 g, 58.5 g, 61.3 g, 59.5 g

Son: 58.1 g, 58.7 g, 59.3 g, 58.9 g, 59.3 g, 58.8 g, 60.4 g, 59.1 g, 59.4 g, 58.9 g, 60.2 g

The packets need to be labelled with the weight. The farmer plans to label them as being 60 g. Is she right to do this? Give your reasons.

Tip

What diagrams and calculations might help you to decide?

The population of the Earth is approximately seven billion (to the nearest billion).

a What is the smallest the population could be?

b What is the largest the population could be?

c If the population of the Earth is p, write down an inequality to represent the range of values that it could take.

One billion = 1 000 000 000. This means that seven billion is 7 000 000 000 people.

d By how many people could the population vary?

Tip

What's the difference between the greatest possible number of people and the smallest possible number of people? You should use your answers to parts **a** and **b** to help you.

Nick has a poster on the wall in his office. Assuming that this poster refers to time, rather than effort, answer the following questions.

ALWAYS GIVE 100%
AT WORK
12% MONDAY
23% TUESDAY
40% WEDNESDAY
20% THURSDAY
5% FRIDAY

Nick's poster

a If Nick actually worked in this way, for how long would he work on a Friday?

b How much longer would Nick work for on a Wednesday compared to a Monday?

Bernard has a similar poster.

ALWAYS GIVE 100%
AT WORK
14% MONDAY
18% TUESDAY
29% WEDNESDAY
36% THURSDAY
3% FRIDAY

Bernard's poster

c Why can't you tell for certain who works for longer on a Tuesday?

You want to buy a mixture of jam and iced doughnuts.

Iced doughnuts cost 15p more than jam doughnuts.

a A jam doughnut costs t pence. Write an expression for the price of an iced doughnut.

You buy 3 jam doughnuts and 5 iced doughnuts. The total cost is £11.95.

b How much does it cost to buy six of each type of doughnut?

The instructions for cooking poultry are: '50 minutes per kilogram plus an additional 30 minutes'.

For Christmas lunch, Fergus needs to cook a 3 kg chicken and a 7.5 kg turkey.

He wants both birds to be ready at the same time and he needs 20 minutes to carve and prepare them, once they are taken out of the oven.

He wants to serve lunch at 1:00 pm on Christmas Day.

a How long will the turkey be in the oven by itself before being joined by the chicken?

b Find a formula to find the time taken, t minutes, to cook a chicken weighing m kg.

For New Year's Day, Fergus plans to cook a goose.

This goose will take 5 hours and 5 minutes to cook.

c How much does the goose weigh?

d If Fergus plans to have a late lunch at 2:30 pm on New Year's Day, what is the latest time he can put the goose in the oven?

The letters in the word MATHEMATICS are written on separate pieces of card and placed in a bag.

a What is the probability that a card chosen randomly from the bag will be a T?

b If this first card is not replaced, what is the probability that the first and second cards will both be T?

The price for laying a lawn is directly proportional to the area of the lawn needed.

For a lawn measuring 8 m by 10 m, there is a charge of £320.

For a lawn measuring 12 m by 12 m, there is a charge of £576.

a How much will it cost to lay a lawn measuring 12 m by 8 m?

b To lay a different lawn costs £560. If the measurements are in whole metres, what could the dimensions of the lawn be?

Twenty years ago Lady Sophia wrote her will. She had a son, twin daughters and a poodle.

Lady Sophia's estate was valued at £5 000 000.

Lady Sophia had decided to leave half of her estate to her son, a third to her daughters to be shared equally between them, and to give the rest to the local pet rescue centre.

a What fraction of the estate would the pet rescue centre have received?

b Express these fractions as a ratio in the order:
son : daughter : daughter : pet rescue centre

c To the nearest thousand pounds, how much would each daughter have received?

Twenty years later, Lady Sophia has spent $\frac{2}{5}$ of her money.

She writes a new will stating that her three children should have $\frac{1}{4}$ of her estate each.

The rest is to be shared equally between her five grandchildren. Lady Sophia is no longer leaving any money to the pet rescue centre.

d How much will each child inherit?

e How much will each grandchild inherit?

Lady Sophia's son will inherit a different amount under the second will to the first.

f Express the two amounts for the son as a ratio.

A butcher always uses the same mix of minced chicken, minced turkey and herbs in his sausages.

For every 4 kg of turkey he adds 7 kg of chicken and 250 g of herbs.

a If the butcher uses 6 kg of minced turkey:

   i how much minced chicken is required?

   ii how many grams of herbs are needed?

b How much turkey would be needed if the butcher used 28 kg of chicken?

c Express the ingredients (herbs : turkey : chicken) in the form: $1 : m : n$.

15 ✪✪☆

At an MK Dons home match against Chelsea, MK Dons had 25 200 supporters in the stadium.

The ratio of home to away supporters was 21 : 4.

a How many Chelsea supporters attended this match?

Four adult tickets were sold for every child's ticket.

b How many children were at the match?

c How many more adults were at the match than children?

During the match, one out of every three children has an ice cream, and 50% of the adults have three soft drinks.

d Calculate how many ice creams are sold.

e Calculate how many soft drinks are sold.

f Express the ratio ice creams : soft drinks in as simple a form as possible.

16 ✪✪☆

The graph shows the journey of a car and a moped.

The moped rider travelled from Edinburgh to Glasgow.

The car driver took the same route to Glasgow but returned to Edinburgh.

a How far did the moped rider travel in the first 25 minutes?

b How long did it take the car to travel the first 10 km? Can you give reasons for the speed for this first stage of the journey?

c How many stops did the moped rider make and what was the total time she spent resting?

d What was the fastest stage of the journey for the car driver?

e What was the driver's speed at this fast stage?

f At approximately what time did the car and the moped pass each other?

g Roughly how far did the moped rider still have to go when she met the car driver?

h What was the average speed for the whole journey for the moped rider?

i What was the average speed for the return journey for the car driver?

Pauline and Emma are two school friends who live in Salford and Woburn Sands, respectively.

The two villages are 18 km apart.

The girls plan to meet up at Emma's house.

Pauline plans to walk directly to Woburn Sands, leaving home at 9:10.

She knows she can walk at a steady speed of 6 kilometres per hour.

Emma's mum plans to leave Woburn Sands at 9:40 to cycle to Salford. She should pass Pauline on her journey.

For the first 16 km, Emma's mum knows she will be travelling fairly fast at 24 km per hour as the road is very flat.

For the rest of the route she has to cycle up a very steep hill and she thinks she will not arrive in Salford until 10:40.

a When will Pauline meet Emma's mum?

b How far will Pauline be from her house when they meet?

c How far will Emma's mum have travelled?

d What time is Pauline expecting to arrive at Emma's house?

e What is the speed that Emma's mum was travelling at when she cycled up the steep hill?

f What distance apart are they at 10:20?

> **Tip**
>
> A graph is likely to be helpful here.

Jenny is shopping for a new television. She discovers that the size advertised is actually the diagonal length of the screen.

Intrigued, she measures her existing TV to see what size it is.

Jenny's measurements are shown on the diagram.

Jenny then attempts to measure the diagonal length of her TV.

She thinks the diagonal length is 80 cm.

Say how you know that Jenny must have measured the diagonal length incorrectly.

32.3 cm

57.7 cm

The price of a second-hand car depends on the mileage.

The prices are calculated using the fact that values are inversely proportional to the mileage.

For a car which has a mileage of 10 000, its price will be £2000.

a Find the formula that is used to price these cars.

b What will be the price of a car that has done 20 000 miles?

c A large red car was priced at £4000. How many miles had this car done?

All standard television screens are mathematically similar.

The size of a TV screen is advertised as the diagonal length, in inches.

Carlos owns a 36.7-inch wide-screen TV.

He measures its width as 32.2 inches.

a What is the aspect ratio (ratio of width to height) for a wide-screen TV?

Eddie is buying a 42-inch wide-screen TV (where 42 inches is the length of the diagonal).

b Work out the length and width of his new TV.

Tip

A diagram will help. Which topic do you need to use?

It is easy to get involved in working on a problem and to forget that you can sometimes use some common sense to tell roughly how big an answer ought to be. You will probably still need to carry out the calculations but this can give you a useful guide as to whether an answer is correct or not.

Here is an advert.

Mike sees the advert above and says "Wow, that's a great deal."

Milly in reply says "I don't think that's possible."

Why is Milly not impressed?

If you estimate that a movie lasts about 2 hours, then you can watch 12 in a full 24 hours. In a week you could watch $12 \times 7 = 84$. You wouldn't get any sleep, though, so you probably wouldn't enjoy them all! You don't need to do any other calculations to see why Milly is unimpressed.

In A-level Biology there are several formulae that are used to calculate the actual size of something which has been viewed through a microscope. It is easy to make a mistake.

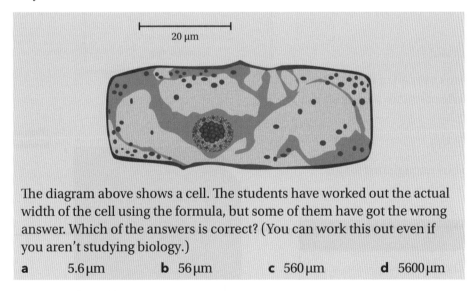

The diagram above shows a cell. The students have worked out the actual width of the cell using the formula, but some of them have got the wrong answer. Which of the answers is correct? (You can work this out even if you aren't studying biology.)

a   5.6 μm   b 56 μm   c 560 μm   d 5600 μm

The line above the diagram is 20 μm long and the cell is about three times as wide as that line, so it must be about 60 μm. The answer must therefore be **b** = 56 μm.

The following problems may be solved using more than one method; however, the worked solutions provided at the back of this book are based on the method introduced above.

Sabina is carrying out a survey on the benefits of exercise. She has created a questionnaire and can't decide who to ask to fill it in. Here are her ideas:

1 The students in her tutor group.

2 The members of her rugby team.

3 Residents of her grandmother's retirement home.

    a For each idea say why there might be a problem.

The diagram below is an extract from Sabina's questionnaire.

How much sport do you do?

◯	◯	◯	◯
1 to 2 hours	2 to 3 hours	3 to 4 hours	4 to 5 hours

    b Write a criticism of the question.

    c Write a criticism of the response section.

What is wrong with this poster?

This is a plan of Nathan's new garden.

Nathan wants to buy turf (grass) to cover all of the garden apart from the patio, which is made of square paving slabs 80 cm in length.

Turf is sold for £2.34 per square metre.

How much will it cost Nathan to buy enough turf for his garden?

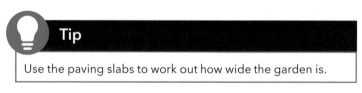

Tip

Use the paving slabs to work out how wide the garden is.

MAY BANK HOLIDAY
SATURDAY/SUNDAY/MONDAY
DEALS FROM

GARY'S GROCERS!

Because this weekend is a third longer

5 m

Diagram not to scale

10.5 m

12 m

PATIO

Rebecca can keep two cows per acre of pasture.

This is a plan of her field.

Diagram not to scale

550 m

90 m

60 m

270 m

Rebecca knows that an acre is an area of about half a football pitch. A football pitch is 68 m by 105 m.

Approximately how many cows can Rebecca keep in her field?

  54.7 × 16.29 ÷ 11.9

Which of the answers below is the best estimate for this calculation?

A 50 **B** 100 **C** 73 **D** 75

> ### Tip
> Remember that you must give reasons for your answer!

Kristie and Amar are both training for the Brighton marathon.

Kristie runs 10 miles each day. Amar runs 15 km each day.

The formula for converting miles to kilometres is: 'Multiply the number of miles by 8 then divide the answer by 5.'

Who do you think will be better prepared for the marathon? Give reasons for your answer.

The ingredients for a chocolate cake that serves eight people are shown below.

Cake	Icing
6 eggs	100 g hazelnuts
125 g unsalted butter	125 ml double cream
400 g chocolate spread	120 g dark chocolate
100 g ground hazelnuts	
150 g dark chocolate	

Fiona has invited 20 guests. She wants to have enough cake for each guest to have one slice.

a How much dark chocolate should Fiona buy?

b The dark chocolate is available in 200 g bars. How many bars will she need?

c Express the amount of chocolate used to chocolate left over as a ratio in its simplest form.

d On another occasion, Fiona reduces the recipe to serve six people. How much chocolate spread does Fiona need?

In London Zoo there are a large number of finches in one big aviary.

The maximum capacity of the aviary is 350 birds so the keeper needs to find out how many birds there are.

He caught 45, put a ring around the leg of each one and put them back in the aviary. A week later he caught 50 finches and found there were 6 with rings already on.

Does the keeper need to find new homes for any of the finches? If so, how many?

Tip

What fraction of the birds have got a ring? How can you work out how many birds there are altogether?

A few students from Year 9 and all of Year 8 are at an outward bounds centre for their school activities week.

One afternoon they can choose to swim, go rock-climbing or go canoeing. The graphs show what they chose.

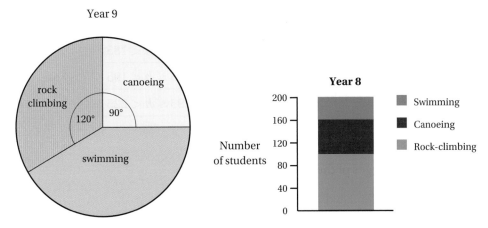

The teacher said that there would be more Year 9 students than Year 8 students in the swimming pools.

Discuss whether this is a correct statement, giving reasons.

Indira asks the boys and girls in her class which pets they own and then makes two pie charts.

Tip

Pie charts like these don't tell us the number of people but instead tell us the proportions.

She now wants to use the pie charts to answer questions such as:

- Do more boys or girls own a dog?
- Are rabbits more likely to be owned by boys or girls?

Why can't she answer these questions from her pie charts?

Two school basketball coaches want to find the average height of all their team members including the reserves.

Coach McKay used the data in the table on the right to find the mean height for his team.

Coach Cooksey used the data below to find the mean height.

150 cm, 156 cm, 187 cm, 199 cm, 203 cm, 178 cm, 194 cm, 188 cm, 167 cm, 194 cm, 152 cm, 226 cm, 225 cm, 199 cm, 188 cm, 221 cm, 178 cm, 143 cm, 142 cm, 170 cm.

a Which coach will have the more accurate mean height for his team? Give reasons for your answer.

b What is the mean height for the McKay team?

c Compare the mean heights and height ranges of the two teams.

Team McKay	
Height (cm)	**Frequency**
$145 \leqslant h < 155$	1
$155 \leqslant h < 165$	2
$165 \leqslant h < 175$	2
$175 \leqslant h < 185$	8
$185 \leqslant h < 195$	3
$195 \leqslant h < 225$	4

Vanessa says that the expression for the area of this rectangle is $x^2 - 7x + 6$.

$x - 6$

$x - 1$

Doug says she is wrong. He says the expression for the area is $2(2x - 7)$.

a Who is correct? Give reasons for your answer.

b What is the expression for the perimeter?

 Put the following in order of size from smallest to largest.

$\sqrt{81}$ $4^2 - 2^3$ $\sqrt[3]{1000}$ $5\sqrt{25} \div 9^0$ $3^{-2} \times 3^2$ $(\sqrt{36})^2$

A fast passenger plane cruises at a constant speed of 1455 miles per hour.

One way to convert miles to kilometres is: 'divide by 5 then multiply by 8'.

a What is the cruising speed of this plane, in kilometres per hour (km/h)?

b At this speed, how long would it take the plane to fly 1746 km?

The distance from Cape Town to London is roughly 9700 km.

Tammy made the journey from Cape Town to London on this fast plane cruising at its normal speed.

c What is the shortest time this journey should take Tammy?

d Say why this time is not possible in reality.

Running tracks come in two standard lengths.

Indoor tracks are 200 m long and outdoor tracks are 400 m long.

a Simon's event is the 1500 m.

How many laps of each track will Simon run in his race?

b Denise will be running both the 5 km and 10 km races.

How many laps of each track will she run in each race?

The rule for working out how long to cook a piece of lamb at 180 °C is: '40 minutes per kg plus 25 minutes'.

a Create a formula to calculate the cooking time for a piece of lamb of any size.

Uncle Bertie wants to serve Sunday lunch at 12:30.

His piece of lamb weighs 3.75 kg and, once taken from the oven, it must stand for 10 minutes before serving.

b Uncle Bertie thinks he needs to put the lamb in the oven at 9 am. Is he right?

Hattie does some form of exercise each day.

Each day she randomly decides to do one of the following: swim 40 lengths, jog 10 km or cycle for 2 hours.

a Draw a sample space diagram showing all the possibilities of the exercise Hattie could do on **two** consecutive days.

b What is the probability that she swims on both days?

c What is the probability that she does not do the same exercise on both days?

A glass of orange squash is $\frac{1}{4}$ squash and the rest water.

A second, identical glass of orange squash is $\frac{5}{6}$ water.

The two glasses are poured into a large drinks bottle.

a What is the fraction of squash in the resulting drink?

Amit is serving drinks at a party. He has two large jugs of fruit punch. The jugs are identical in size, but one contains punch that is $\frac{2}{5}$ apple juice and the other contains punch that is $\frac{3}{10}$ apple juice.

b Amit wonders how the drink will change if he pours some from both jugs into a glass.

Is it possible for Amit to create a drink that is exactly $\frac{1}{2}$ apple juice?

> **Tip**
>
> The strength of the squash in the answer should be between the two strengths in the question.

A health campaign is targeting the high levels of sugar in low-fat foods.

One particular brand of low-fat yogurt is sold in 104 g pots and contains 5.9 g of sugar.

Another yogurt, is sold in 90 g pots and contains 5% sugar.

a Which yogurt contains more sugar?

b If the guideline daily amount (GDA) of sugar for an adult is approximately 90 g, how do the two yogurts compare?

In astronomy, distances are commonly measured in 'Astronomical Units' (AU). 1 AU is the average distance from the Sun to the Earth. 1 AU = 9.3×10^7 miles.

Planet	Distance from Sun in AU
Mercury	0.387
Venus	0.723
Earth	1.000
Mars	1.524
Jupiter	5.203
Saturn	9.523
Uranus	19.208
Neptune	30.087

a Which pair of planets has the shortest possible distance between them?

b What is that distance in miles?

Peter is 2.03 m tall. He and his three shorter friends are planning on going camping.

They will be using a traditional tent in the shape of a triangular prism.

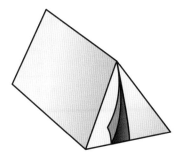

What dimensions must their tent be if Peter is to be able to comfortably stand upright and lie flat to sleep alongside his three friends?

Tip

You will need to make some assumptions in order to answer this question. You know how tall Peter is but how much space will he need from side to side?

Sometimes it's useful to make a change to a diagram or scenario so that it is easier to see what's going on.

Here is an example.

The diagram shows a red square with a purple circle drawn through its vertices and a blue square drawn so it touches the purple circle on all sides.

What is the relationship between the area of the red square and the area of the blue square? Give reasons for how you know.

Before you turn the page, have a go at the question.

What ideas have you got?

Here are some things you can try.

- Get a rough idea of what the answer will be; you know that the blue square is bigger than the red square, but it is certainly less than, say, four times the area. This is not the way to work out the final answer, not least because you can't provide an explanation, but it will help you decide if your answer seems reasonable later.
- You don't know any measurements, so do you need to provide some?
- Will it help to call the side length of the red square *x*? Or the radius of the circle could be *r*. Maybe this will be useful and maybe it won't.
- Try putting on some extra lines. Will they help?

Tip

If you can't do it, please don't worry. This is a mathematical problem that is supposed to be difficult. Remember, if you can just 'see' the answer then it wouldn't be a mathematical 'problem'.

Did you manage to answer the problem?

If not, here's one way that you could have solved it by changing the way you look at the diagram.

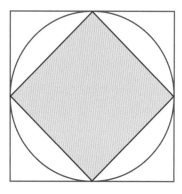

If you rotate the red square nothing vital changes.

The area of the red square is still the same and the purple and blue shapes are unaffected.

Does this help you to see the relationship between the red square and the blue square?

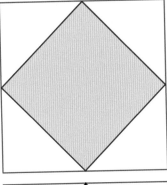

To make this very clear you can remove the circle.

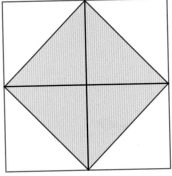

Then you can divide the shape up like this.

Tip

The extra lines are helpful after you've rotated the red square.

Now you can say why the area of the red square is half the area of the blue square. Here is an example of a full answer.

If you rotate the red square so the vertices of the red square meet the middle of the sides of the blue square you do not change its area.

The two extra lines I have added join the vertices of the red square, cutting it into quarters that are right-angled triangles. These lines also join the middle of the sides of the blue square, cutting it into quarters that are squares.

The total area of the red right-angled triangles is half the area of the blue square.

So the area of the red square is half the area of the blue square.

The following problems may be solved using more than one method; however, the worked solutions provided at the back of this book are based on the method introduced above.

Tip

You had a rough idea that the area of the blue square is between one and four times the area of the red square, and it is. Estimating the answer can be a useful check that your final answer is sensible.

Tip

You might have answered this question by working out some measurements in terms of *x* or *r* instead of using this method. This is also a good way to solve the problem.

Candice has a favourite set of colouring pencils. Some are well-used and have been sharpened many times.

The lengths of her pencils are:

12.5 cm, 11 cm, 11.2 cm, 9 cm, 8.4 cm, 8.7 cm, 6.9 cm, 7.4 cm, 11 cm, 10.7 cm, 11.4 cm and 9.8 cm.

Candice's mother has said that she can have a new set of colouring pencils when the average length of her pencils is less than 10 cm.

If she wants to get new pencils, should Candice tell her mother the modal length, the median length or the mean length?

A spinner has 12 equal sections.

The probability of getting purple is $\frac{1}{3}$, red is $\frac{1}{6}$ and green is $\frac{1}{12}$.

All other sections are coloured blue.

How many blue sections are there?

A special eight-sided dice has some of its numbers repeated.

Here is some information about the numbers on the dice:

i All of the numbers are less than 5.

ii All of the numbers are positive integers.

iii The probability of rolling a 1 is $\frac{1}{8}$.

iv The probability of rolling a multiple of 2 is $\frac{3}{4}$.

v The probability of rolling a square number is $\frac{3}{8}$.

What is the probability of rolling a prime number?

a What is the probability of throwing a six on an ordinary fair dice?

Bashir told Aaron that if he threw a dice twelve times he should get two sixes.

b Is Bashir correct? Give reasons for your answer.

 Tip

Think about your reasons and think of alternative arguments.

Ben and John are both in the school cricket team.

In the last match Ben made 17 runs.

John came up with this formula for the number of runs he made in the same match. "To work out my number of runs, multiply Ben's number of runs by 3, then subtract 14."

a How many runs did John make in that particular match?

b If this formula worked for every match, who would you consider the better cricketer? Say why.

c When would this formula fail to work? Say why.

Tip

Try a big number and then try a small number. What is going on?

Jenny is given a set of instructions to create an image.

1 Mark a point on your page and label it 'O'.

2 Draw a 1 cm square with its bottom left-hand corner 1 cm to the right of O.

3 Enlarge this square by a scale factor of 2 about O.

4 Translate the smaller square 1 cm to the left.

5 Rotate the two smaller squares 90° clockwise about the centre of the larger square.

6 Rotate the image (up to and including step 5) 180° about the centre of the larger square.

a What should Jenny's completed image look like?

b How many lines of symmetry does the resulting image have?

c What order of rotational symmetry does the resulting image have?

d Design a set of instructions to create the image below.

Tip

There are more than 16.

Here is an equilateral triangle.

a How many triangles, similar to the equilateral triangle above, are there in this next diagram?

b Give reasons for your answer.

The top row of the table shows three views of the trapezium-prism.

For 3-D solids A, B and C two of the views are given. Draw the top view for each one.

	Front view	Right view	Top view
A			
B			
C			

Compare each pair of numbers and decide which symbol out of <, >, or = should be placed in between them.

a $\dfrac{2}{3}$ 0.66

b 0.25 $\dfrac{8}{32}$

c $\dfrac{3}{11}$ 0.273

d 0.05 $\dfrac{1}{22}$

e 0.5   0.4999... (repeating 9s)

A teacher has asked his class to invent a riddle to describe a polygon of their choice.

This is Jillian's riddle.

I have a prime number of sides.
All of my interior angles are obtuse.
I have rotational symmetry of order 5.
What am I?

a Which polygon is Jillian describing?

Give as specific an answer as possible.

Gemma hasn't finished her riddle. So far she has the following:

I am a quadrilateral.
I have two pairs of parallel sides.

b Say which four quadrilaterals Gemma could be referring to.

c Write a final clue for the riddle that means there is just one answer.
Can you do this for all of the possible answers?

Andy is looking for his homework about regular polygons. This is what he can see on his desk.
As you can see, Andy's work is partially covered by a piece of paper.

a Which regular polygon will Andy reveal when he lifts the piece of paper?

Andy wonders how difficult it would be to identify other polygons that have been partially covered.

b Which regular polygon could be hidden under each of these pieces of paper?

Terri is making a birthday cake for her friend.

She will write 'Happy Birthday' in icing on the top.

She makes a template for the letters, on centimetre-squared paper, as shown below.

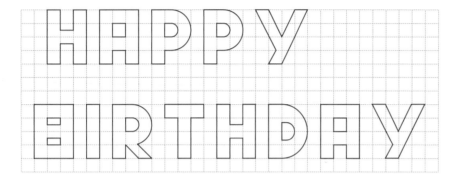

a What is the area of the letter H?

b What is the area of the letter Y?

c Does the letter B have a greater area than the letter D?

d Which letter has the smallest area? How do you know?

> **Tip**
>
> Try to divide the letters up into more familiar shapes. There's more than one way to do this. Try it out and see what works for you.

Sections of decorative fencing are made with metal and wooden rods.

——— Metal rod
▬▬ Wooden rod

a How many metal rods will be needed in the next pattern?

b How many wooden rods are needed for the fourth pattern?

c Find the number of metal rods needed for the nth pattern (the nth term).

The metal rods cost £2 each and the wooden rods cost £2.50 each.

d Sue needs a fence consisting of 12 sections.

How much will this cost her?

The two plan views below were provided in a test paper.

A Circle   **B** Square

Students had to give the names of the 3-D shapes that these plans were from. The results are shown in the table below.

Name	Shape A	Shape B
Matt	cylinder	cube
Jeremy	cone	cuboid
Niall	sphere	cylinder

Who was correct?

100 people were asked to complete a questionnaire about their pets.

Out of the 100 people, 17 had both a cat and a dog.

A total of 54 had either a cat or a dog, but not both.

30 people owned a dog.

a If one person was chosen at random, what is the probability they had neither a cat nor a dog?

b If one person was chosen at random, what is the probability they only owned a cat?

Simon is a landscape gardener and he needs to hire a small digger for his next job.

The cost of hiring a digger from JCEs is shown as a straight-line graph.

MoveIt Builders also hire out diggers but they have a basic fixed charge in addition to their daily charge. Their charges are also shown as a straight-line graph.

a Which graph line refers to the charges for which company?

b What is the basic fixed charge made by one of the companies?

c How much per day does JCEs charge?

d Is MoveIt Builders' daily charge more or less than what JCEs charge? By how much?

e What would be the total cost if Simon hired the digger from MoveIt Builders for 5 days?

f What would be the total charge if Simon needed the digger for two weeks and he hired it from MoveIt Builders?

g If Simon needed the digger for two weeks, would it be cheaper from MoveIt Builders or JCEs?

h For the two-week period, how much less would it cost to hire from the cheaper company?

Triangles ABC and XYZ are similar shapes.

In triangle ABC, length AB is 8 cm and AC is 20 cm.

In triangle XYZ, length XY is 14 cm.

 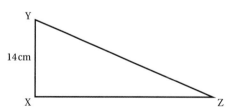

a What is the length of XZ?

b Work out the area of triangle ABC and triangle XYZ.

c Express area of triangle ABC : area of triangle XYZ in its simplest form.

d What type of numbers are in the ratio? Can you give reasons for this?

18

Arthur has just bought a circular dining table of diameter 240 cm.

It comes flat-packed to make it easier to transport.

Arthur's front door is rectangular and is 2.1 m tall and 1.05 m wide.

Will he be able to fit the table-top through the door?

Tip

It should be clear that the circular table is not going to fit through the door if held vertically or horizontally. Arthur will need to tilt it to try to get it inside.

19

Would you rather:

a receive 80% of £10 or 75% of £12?

b do homework for 20% of 1 hour or $\frac{3}{8}$ of half an hour?

c have 50% of one chocolate cake or 25% of two chocolate cakes?

d buy a CD in store for £12.99 or buy it online with a 5% discount code but a postage charge of £1.99?

Tip

You could work out the answer to each calculation, but is there an alternative method for some of them?

20

 Two rectangles are shown below. They are not drawn to scale.

A

$(2^2)^2$

$3\sqrt[4]{81}$

B

5^2

$\sqrt{4}$

Tip

Try to simplify the side lengths of the rectangles. If you can write them as ordinary numbers the problem will be much simpler.

a Which rectangle has the greater perimeter?

b Which has the greater area?

21

Aaron went to the local fruit market and bought four apples and five bananas for £2.05.

Peter went to the same fruit market and bought three apples and seven bananas for £2.35.

Aaron and Peter asked their maths teacher for an easy method to find the price of an apple and the price of a banana.

She told them they could create an equation for the cost of the fruit each of them bought and solve them simultaneously.

a Write the two equations.

b What is the price of one apple?

c What is the price of a banana?

22

> **Tip**
>
> You cut the border into sections and work out the area of each section using algebra.

a Create a formula, in terms of x, to calculate the area of the shaded border.

b The area of the border is $204\,\text{cm}^2$.

What are the dimensions of the outer rectangle?

23

Anna is planning to do something silly to raise money for charity.

She wants to take a bath in cola and wants to know how many bottles of it she will need to buy.

> **Tip**
>
> Remember: $1\,\text{ml} = 1\,\text{cm}^3$.

Anna starts by converting the volume of the bath tub from m^3 into cm^3. She says: "There's $100\,\text{cm}$ in $1\,\text{m}$ so I just need to multiply by 100. $0.15\,\text{m}^3 = 15\,\text{cm}^3$."

a Say why Anna is wrong. Her bath tub does **not** have a volume of $15\,\text{cm}^3$.

b Calculate the actual volume of the bath tub in cm^3.

c Calculate the number of litres of cola Anna will need to buy.

In how many ways can you get from flag **A** to flag **B** as shown in the diagram:

a using a single transformation?

b using exactly two transformations?

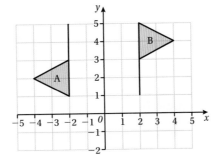

Tip

Remember to provide all of the information necessary to fully describe each transformation.

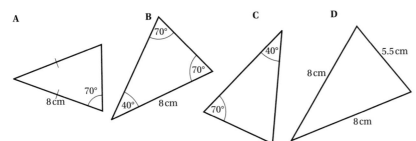

Which of the statements about these triangles are definitely true?

a All four triangles are congruent.

b None of the triangles are congruent.

c Triangles A, B and C are congruent.

d Triangles B and C are congruent.

e Triangles A and B are congruent.

Tip

Remember to refer to the conditions for congruence.

In some problems you need to make sure you get every possible answer, without missing any or getting the same answer twice.

Here is the flag of South Korea.

Around the edge of the central circle there are four 'trigrams'. These are made up of three lines. The one on the right has three solid lines.

And this one has a broken line at the bottom and the top, with a solid line in the middle.

If you just use solid lines and broken lines, what fraction of all the possible trigrams (made using three lines) appear on the South Korean flag?

First of all, do you understand the problem? There are other trigrams that haven't yet been drawn, such as the one on the right.

It looks as if you will need to work out how many possibilities there are. If you just start writing them down (which is a reasonable starting point) there is a risk that you will miss some of them, or maybe write the same one twice.

These are the ones you have got so far.

A better way to solve this problem would be to work systematically. You could start with three solid lines and no broken lines. That is easy because there is only one of them, as shown on the right.

Next you could have two solid lines and one broken line.

This example is systematic in the way the broken line has moved downwards. Can you finish off the rest of the trigrams?

The final list that you get is as follows.

There are eight of them and you can be confident that because you have worked systematically you haven't missed any out, or got any of them twice. Go back to the original question: **What fraction of all the possible trigrams (made using three lines) appear on the South Korean flag?**

There are four of them on the flag and you know there are eight altogether, so $\frac{1}{2}$ of the trigrams appear on the flag. (Rather neatly, they have chosen to use the four that look the same, both ways up!) If you want to test out your ability to work systematically you could try to find all of the ways to make a diagram that uses four lines.

Here is another problem that can be solved by working systematically.

> Without using a calculator decide whether 40 735 982 is a square number or not.

Finding the square root of a large number without using a calculator or computer is difficult.

You could start by making a list of square numbers (as in the table):

That's interesting: the final digit is the same in each row (for example 7^2 and 17^2 both end in 9).

Can you say why that must always happen?

The number in question is 40 735 98<u>2</u>. You are looking for a number that ends in a 2. But there aren't any (all square numbers end in either 0, 1, 4, 5, 6 or 9), so 40 735 982 isn't a square number.

(If it ended in a 0, 1, 4, 5, 6, or 9 you would need to do some more tests to find out whether it is square.)

The following problems may be solved using more than one method; however, the worked solutions provided at the back of this book are based on the method introduced above.

n	Square number (n^2)	n	Square number (n^2)
1	1	11	121
2	4	12	144
3	9	13	169
4	16	14	196
5	25	15	225
6	36	16	256
7	49	17	289
8	64	18	324
9	81	19	361
10	100	20	400

The first two questions on a worksheet are shown in the diagram below.

```
    1           4
  + 3         + 5
  _____       _____

  _____       _____
```

> **Tip**
>
> Think about how you can be sure that you have considered every possible combination of two integers. You might like to use an addition square to organise these.

a Using positive integers less than 10, how many different addition questions like this could be on the rest of the worksheet? (Note that the order in addition is not important, so 1 + 3 is the same as 3 + 1, therefore these do not count as different questions.)

b If another worksheet only includes negative integers greater than –10, how many **different answers** to addition calculations could there be?

In this problem, you are only allowed to add the numbers 3 and 5. You can add as many of them as you want. For example, you can make 13 by adding 3 + 5 + 5.

What is the largest number you **cannot** make in this way?

Which number under 18 has the most factors?

The tiles on a kitchen floor are regular hexagons of side length 130 mm.

a Calculate the perimeter of the shaded section of tiles in the diagram below. Give your answer in centimetres (cm).

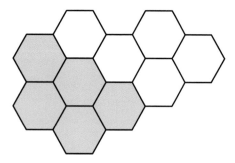

b A different section of tiles has a perimeter of 156 cm. How many tiles are there in this section?

> **Tip**
>
> You could use triangular dotted paper to help you draw the hexagons.

Charmaine makes bracelets. These include flowers made with pink beads and blue beads.

Each flower consists of one pink bead surrounded by six blue beads.

The number of flowers she puts on a bracelet depends on the size of the bracelet.

a How many blue beads would she need for a bracelet with three pink beads?

b The number of blue beads follows a pattern. What is the nth term for this pattern?

Connor rolls a biased dice 50 times and gets 15 sixes.

a How many sixes should he expect if he rolls the dice 100 times?

b After many rolls Connor has recorded 105 sixes; how many times do you think he has rolled the dice?

c How many sixes should he expect if he rolls the dice 1200 times?

 Look at each pair of multiplications below and decide in each case which of the pair gives the **larger** answer.

a 10×7 or 11×6

b -44×5 or 44×-5

c $972\,310 \times 0$ or 1×1

d 91×-2 or 59×3

$5\,\square\,2\,\square\,10\,\square\,-3$

Insert the operators: +, −, and × into the three boxes above. You should use all of them once each.

In how many ways can you achieve a negative result?

> **Tip**
>
> In how many ways can you arrange the three operators in the spaces provided? Can you find a systematic way of recording all of the possible arrangements to be sure that you've considered them all?

 Which of the following calculations has the smallest answer?

i $100 \div (5^2 \times 2)$ **ii** $620 \times 4 \div 248$

iii $81 - 37 \times 2$ **iv** $-27 \div -3 + 12$

Three students are asked the question: **What is the smallest integer that is exactly divisible by 2 and 3?**

The students give three correct answers to this question:

Gemma says: "It must be 6 because $2 \times 3 = 6$."

Lidia says: "It must be 6 because it can't be 4 (3 doesn't work); it can't be 5 (2 and 3 both don't work), but it can be 6."

Harry says: "It must be 6 because the 2 times table goes: 2, 4, 6, 8, ..., and the 3 times table goes: 3, 6, 9, ... So 6 is the first number that is in both lists."

Students are then asked the question: **What is the smallest integer that is exactly divisible by 2, 3 and 4?**

a i What would Gemma's answer be (assuming she used the same method as above)?

   ii Is Gemma correct?

   iii Would Lidia or Harry be correct if they applied their methods?

   iv Can you think of another method to answer this question?

A final question is asked: **What is the smallest integer that is exactly divisible by 3, 5 and 6?**

b Select an approach from the methods given above to help you to solve this problem.

Martin helps himself to sandwiches from a buffet lunch. He notices that the sandwiches have all been cut into identical triangles.

Martin realises that he has placed four sandwiches so that they fit together to create a square.

He wonders how many different polygons he can create by arranging two or more sandwiches on his plate.

a Assuming that Martin matches the edges of the sandwiches, how many different polygons can he create, using:

   i exactly two sandwiches

   ii exactly three sandwiches

   iii all four sandwiches?

b Is it possible for Martin to create all of the special types of quadrilateral, using two or more sandwiches from his plate?

 Tip

Think of a logical way of trying out all of the possible arrangements of the sandwiches.
You also need to decide upon a sensible way of recording your findings so that you can be sure you have found **all** of the possible polygons.
Where possible, try to use the correct mathematical name for each polygon that you find.

A factory makes packing boxes for cylinders.

Each box is a cuboid measuring 40 cm by 40 cm with a height of 15 cm.

a What are the maximum dimensions (radius and height) of the cylinders that can fit into each box?

b Make a guess as to which box has the most unused space.

c Use calculations to check your guess. What did you find?

> **Tip**
>
> The volume of a cylinder is $\pi \times r^2 \times h$.

In a school's packed lunch, students can have a sandwich and either crisps, fruit or a yogurt, plus a bottle of water or carton of fruit juice.

a List all the different combinations of packed lunches available.

b Kai randomly picks up a packed lunch. What is the probability that Kai's packed lunch will have a yogurt?

c If each combination of lunch has an equally likely chance of being prepared, how many of the 330 children on a school trip will have crisps in their packed lunch?

Tania is asked to randomly think of a number greater than 1 but less than 50.

What is the probability that the number Tania chooses is:

a an even number? **b** an odd number?

c a multiple of 5? **d** the number 27?

e a factor of 48?

In Ahmed's money box there is a total of £47 and this includes twelve 50p coins and nine £1 coins. The rest of the coins are £2 coins.

Ahmed wants to shake one coin out of his money box.

What is the probability that it will be a £2 coin?

Timi's dad has two sets of jelly moulds. In one set he has a circle, star and triangle mould. In the other set he has a heart, a rabbit and a car.

Timi wants his dad to make him some jelly using one mould from each set.

a Show all the different combinations Timi could have.

b Timi's dad randomly picks a mould from each set. What is the probability that he will pick the star and the rabbit?

Julie has eight black pens, one red pen and three blue pens in her pencil case.

Julie needs a pen, so she randomly picks one from her pencil case.

a What is the probability that it is a blue pen?

Julie puts her pen back in her pencil case.

In the next lesson, Julie needs a pen again and Tommy wants to borrow one as well.

Julie randomly picks a pen from her pencil case for herself and one for Tommy.

b What is the probability that both Julie and Tommy get a blue pen?

Max has 12 panels of fencing that he will join together to make a run for his pet rabbits.

Each panel is 60 cm long.

He arranges them so that they enclose a square.

a What is the area of the pen that Max has created?

Adam thinks he can make the run larger by rearranging the panels into a rectangle, where the length is double the width.

b Is Adam correct?

Kim thinks she can make the run larger by rearranging the panels into an equilateral triangle.

c Is Kim right?

Tip

Remember, you must always give reasons for your answer. Make sure that someone reading it will be convinced.

Four similar triangles are placed together to form the pattern shown below.

Diagram not to scale

1

1

a Show that the area of the largest triangle is 4 times that of the smallest triangle.

b Do the four triangles meet on a straight line?

Tip

You have right-angled triangles in the image. Remember that you can use Pythagoras' theorem and trigonometry in right-angled triangles.

Find values for a, b and c that make the following equation true.

$$245 = 1^a + 2^b + 3^c$$

Tip

You might like to start by trying out some numbers in place of a, b and c.
Remember that you are trying to make 245, so it might help if you wrote out the first few powers of 1, 2 and 3 so that you can get a feel for the size of the numbers that might be needed.

There is a strange scenario that exists if you are having difficulties with a problem. You could call it 'The problem with problem solving' as shown in this diagram.

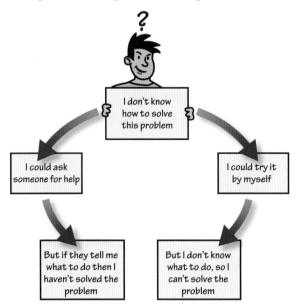

So if you find yourself in this situation, one strategy you could try is: 'If you don't know what to do, do something.' But make sure the 'something' you do is useful.

Some things that are **not** useful might include colouring a picture (unless it is a problem about colouring), or writing the question out in perfect handwriting. These are just things that keep you busy, but which are unlikely to help.

The previous chapters in this book outlined different problem-solving strategies. If you don't know what to do for a question, try one of these strategies. If the first one you try doesn't work, try a different strategy.

You might find it helpful to write down the things you do know (for example, the key ideas from the question) and which areas of mathematics these relate to.

Here is an example.

> Ben bought a bag of rice at the supermarket. He wonders how many grains of rice there are in the bag. Can you help him?

There are all sorts of things that seem to make this question impossible to answer.

- Not every bag of rice has exactly the same number of grains of rice in it.
- Different varieties of rice are different sizes (for example, long grain rice is longer than risotto rice).
- Individual grains vary in size.
- We don't know how big the bag is. If he has bought a 1 kg bag then there will be approximately twice as many grains as there will be in a 500 g bag.

You will have realised by now that there isn't going to be an exact answer, so you need to work out a rough answer. It is often useful to work out a ball-park figure, and as long as it is of the right order of magnitude (which means it has roughly the correct number of digits) then that will be reasonable.

If you decide a problem is difficult and do nothing then it won't get solved! You could start to try some things that might be useful.

Count every grain of rice in a bag.

Nice idea, but you haven't got a bag of rice and the answer is probably rather big, so it will take a long time and that involves counting rather than doing maths, so let's try something else.

Weigh a single grain and then work out how many grains there will be in 1 kg.

This is nicer, no counting involved! A 2p coin weighs 7 g, so a single grain of rice will be extremely light, and certainly less than 1 g. Your scales aren't accurate enough to do this though (and you don't have any rice to weigh anyway).

Find out how many grains weigh 1 g and then multiply by 1000.

This is useful because it uses the fact that 1000 g = 1 kg. But you still don't have any rice to weigh.

Find out how big a grain of rice is.

Can you draw a picture of an uncooked grain of rice? (Uncooked rice is smaller than the fluffy, cooked rice.) In this drawing the grain is about half a cm long and maybe 2 mm high.

What shape is a grain of rice?

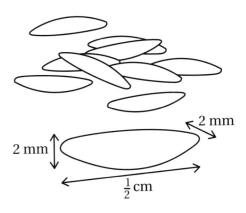

It's a bit like a cylinder but with sloping ends. In fact, it is roughly a cuboid! You could work out the rough volume of the grain of rice by assuming it is a cuboid that is $\frac{1}{2}$ cm by 2 mm by 2 mm.

Work out the volume of a bag of rice and compare this to the volume of a grain of rice. In the kitchen cupboard at home you are probably used to seeing 1 kg bags of food (sugar, flour, pasta, rice, and so on). You can get a mental image of a 1 kg bag of sugar, using your ruler to help visualise the size, which is about 10 cm by 15 cm by 8 cm.

But the units are all different. That is awkward, so you could work in mm.

The volume of a single grain of rice is about 5 mm × 2 mm × 2 mm. This is 20 mm³.

The volume of the bag is about 100 mm × 150 mm × 80 mm. This is 1 200 000 mm³.

1 200 000 ÷ 20 = 60 000, so you could estimate there are roughly 60 000 grains in a bag.

Ask yourself, does this seem reasonable?

If 60 000 grains of rice weigh 1 kg then about 60 of them would weigh 1 g. So this does seem possible. The errors in your estimate of the sizes are likely to be outweighed by the fact that rice grains are not cuboids, but they also don't fit together perfectly in the bag.

To start with we had no idea what to do. We tried out some different ideas and eventually worked out an answer.

The following problems may be solved using more than one method; however, the worked solutions provided at the back of this book are based on the method introduced above.

1

Dance United are touring America. They are a group of 15 dancers and they need to pay as little as possible for hotel rooms.

In America there is a chain of motels that use the following formula for their room charges: '$75 for one person plus $35 per extra person'. In Dallas, the motel only has rooms with three beds.

In Las Vegas, the motel has rooms with four beds.

In San Francisco, there were only two rooms left that had six beds; the rest of the rooms had two beds.

a How much did the accommodation cost in Dallas?

b How much cheaper was it to stay in Las Vegas, compared to Dallas?

c Which was the cheapest city for the dancers to stay in?

2

Jenny watched a fitness group running laps of the playing field shown in the diagram below. Most people completed three laps before stopping.

a How far did most people run? Give your answer in kilometres.

Two of the runners continued for another four laps.

b How far did those two people run? Give your answer in kilometres.

> **Tip**
>
> Remember: 1000 m = 1 km.

3

Sarah knows her height is 5 ft 10 inches.

Leon's height is 180 cm and he tells Sarah he is taller than she is.

Given that 1 inch is approximately the same as 2.5 cm, is Leon correct?

4

Tarjhay was given £40 for his birthday and he really wanted to buy his favourite basketball team's kit.

The kit costs $65.

The exchange rate at the time was £1 = $1.70.

How much money will he have left?

Jyoti and Indira are making towers with cubes.

Between them they have 12 cubes, each of different sizes.

There is a 1 cm cube, a 2 cm cube, a 3 cm cube, a 4 cm cube and so on, up to the biggest cube, which measures 12 cm along each edge.

For the first towers they make, Jyoti uses the six smallest cubes and Indira uses the six largest.

a How much taller is Indira's tower compared to Jyoti's?

The girls then decide to make two towers of the same height, each using cubes.

b Work out a combination of cubes that each girl could have.

For a set of eight whole numbers, the following information is known:

- The biggest number is 16.
- Mean = 7.5.
- Mode = 3 and 5.
- Range = 15.

What could the numbers be?

> **Tip**
>
> There is more than one answer.

Which of the statements about the number 12 345 678 912 are true?

i It is a multiple of 3.

ii It is a prime number.

iii Dividing the number by 5 leaves a remainder of 2.

iv It is a multiple of 4.

> **Tip**
>
> How can you quickly decide if a number is a multiple of 3, a multiple of 4 or a multiple of 9?

Grandad Jones is twice as old as his son Geoff. Geoff is 28 years older than his son Paul.

The total of the ages of the three family members is 112 years.

What ages are Grandad Jones, Geoff and Paul?

The formula for calculating the cost of placing an advert in a local newspaper is $c = 17n + 60$ where n is the number of words and c is the cost, in pence.

a Find the cost of an advert which contains 55 words.

b Sally placed an advert and it cost £21. How many words did Sally's advert have?

Jolene wants to place an advert to try to sell her bicycle. She does not want to spend more than £10 on her advert.

c What is the maximum number of words Jolene can use to keep the cost to £10 or less?

Mo is running a marathon this weekend. He will carry a water bottle as shown in the diagram below. He has bought some energy powder that dissolves in water.

15 cm

8 cm

To the nearest half-scoop, how many scoops of the energy powder should he use to make a full bottle of energy drink?

Tip

Remember: 1 cm³ = 1 ml.

For every eight students going on a school trip there must be an accompanying teacher.

A school trip is planned for 140 students.

a How many teachers will need to be on this trip?

Extra teachers want to join the trip.

There are now 21 teachers available for the trip.

b How many extra students could go on the trip?

It was too late to take extra students, so the original 140 students went with the extra teachers.

c What is the new ratio of students to teachers?

Harvey translated a shape by the vector $\begin{pmatrix} 2 \\ 3 \end{pmatrix}$ and got the image shown in the diagram below.

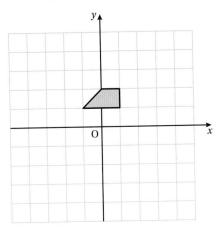

a Where was Harvey's original shape?

Harvey rotated another shape 90° clockwise about the origin and got the second image.

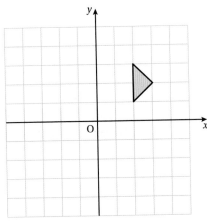

b Where was Harvey's original shape?

Harvey rotated a further shape 90° anti-clockwise about (1, 1), and then translated it by the vector $\begin{pmatrix} -3 \\ 2 \end{pmatrix}$ to achieve the final image shown.

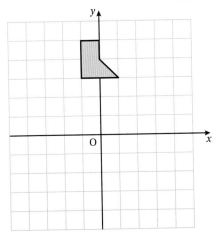

c Where was Harvey's original shape?

Tip

How can you work backwards through this problem? What are the 'inverse' transformations that need to be applied?

13

 A magic square has the property that the numbers in each row, column and diagonal add up to the same thing (the 'Magic Number').

For the magic square shown below, the Magic Number is 2.1.

0.74		
$\frac{129}{150}$		
		$\frac{33}{50}$

Copy and complete the magic square.

14

There are approximately 5×10^9 red blood cells per millilitre of blood. James's blood volume is 9 pints.

One pint is equal to 568 ml.

If James donates 10% of his blood, how many red blood cells does he have left?

15

Flo visits a garden centre. She buys a wooden planter box.

The planter is in the shape of a cuboid and measures 1 m × 80 cm × 70 cm.

She also buys compost to fill the planter box.

Compost is sold in 50 litre bags.

a What is the smallest number of bags of compost Flo needs to buy to fill the planter completely?

The bags of compost cost £5.99 each and are also on a special offer: 3 for £12.

b How much will it cost for Flo to buy the compost?

c How much money does Flo save by taking advantage of the special offer?

Tip

Remember:
1 cm³ = 1 ml
1 litre = 1000 ml

Female rabbits can have from four to eight kits (baby rabbits) per litter.

The probability of a pregnant female rabbit having a given number of kits per litter is given in the table.

Number of kits per litter	4	5	6	7	8
Probability	0.1	0.2	0.3	0.3	x

a   What is the probability that a randomly picked pregnant female rabbit will have eight kits in one litter?

b   What is the probability that two randomly picked pregnant female rabbits have a total of 16 kits in one breeding season?

c   What is the probability that two randomly picked pregnant female rabbits have a total of 10 kits in one breeding season?

A field is 80 m long by 70 m wide.

A goat is tethered to a pole in the centre of the field using a rope 15 m long.

A farmer plants wheat across the width of the field for 30 m from one end. The goat eats all the wheat it can reach.

Draw a scale drawing and shade the area of wheat the goat eats.

Two identical triangles are drawn using two diameters and two vertical lines inside a circle of radius 7 cm as shown.

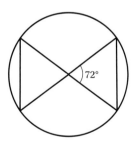

If this diagram is placed on a 1 cm coordinate grid so that the centre of the circle is located at the origin, what will be the coordinates of points **A** and **B**?

 Tip

You have a right-angled triangle, another angle and a side length. What topic can you use?

1

	Hot chocolate	Tea	Coffee	Total
Women	**8**	9	**12**	29
Men	8	7	10	**25**
Total	16	**16**	22	54

> A diagram like this 2-way table will help here.

> The bold numbers are given in the question and the rest can be worked out.

Of the 54 workers surveyed, 22 preferred coffee, 16 preferred tea and 16 preferred hot chocolate.

Peter was incorrect. Tea is not the most popular drink; coffee is the most popular hot drink among the workers, and hot chocolate is as popular as tea.

2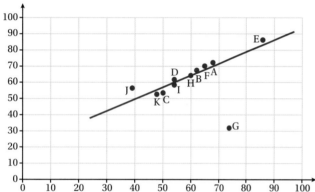

> An easy way to see what is going on is to draw a scatter graph.

> Then draw a line of best fit on the scatter graph.

a The line of best fit suggests that a mark of 70 in Statistics would link with a mark of about 66 in Mathematics.

b This is a very good positive correlation, so the prediction is likely to be fairly accurate.

c Student G is an outlier.

3 **a**

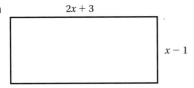

The perimeter = $2x + 3 + x - 1 + 2x + 3 + x - 1$

$= 6x + 4$

To work out the perimeter of a rectangle, you need to add up the sides.

A diagram will help.

b The perimeter is 70 cm, so $6x + 4 = 70$.

$x = 11$

The longest side is $2x + 3 = 2 \times 11 + 3$, which is 25 cm.

Solve $6x + 4 = 70$ for x.

c The width is $x - 1 = 11 - 1$, which is 10 cm.

The area is therefore $25 \times 10 = 120\,\text{cm}^2$.

To work out the area of a rectangle you multiply the length and the width. This means you need to work out the width.

4 Top cylinder:

Draw a diagram of the top cylinder.

When this is cut along the dotted line it can be unwrapped to give a rectangle, where the height of the rectangle is the same as the height of the cylinder and the width is the same as the circumference of the cylinder. The diagram helps to show what is going on.

Surface area of the top cylinder is $\pi \times 28 \times 15 = 420\pi$
$(= 1319.4689...\,\text{cm}^2)$

Work out the area of each rectangle.

The middle one is $\pi \times 22 \times 10 = 220\pi$
$(= 691.15038...\,\text{cm}^2)$

The lowest one is $\pi \times 16 \times 10 = 160\pi$
$(= 502.65482...\,\text{cm}^2)$

The total is therefore $420\pi + 220\pi + 160\pi = 800\pi$
$= 2513.3\,\text{cm}^2$ (1 dp)

Add up the three areas.

Round your answer to one decimal place (dp).

5

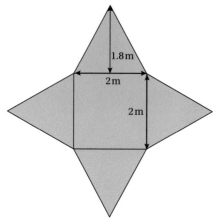

> A diagram shows all of the shapes. The triangles are all the same.

Area of base = 2 m × 2 m = 4 m²

Area of one triangular face = $\frac{1}{2}$ × 2 m × 1.8 m = 1.8 m²

Area of four triangular faces = 1.8 m² × 4 = 7.2 m²

Total area = 4 m² + 7.2 m² = 11.2 m²

> Area of square base = length × width.

> Area of one triangular face = $\frac{1}{2}$ base × height.

> Total surface area of tent
> (square base + four triangular faces).

6

Lavender

Geranium

> Draw a diagram of two of the rows.

There must be 7 rows of geraniums (70 ÷ 10 = 7), so there are 8 rows of lavender because it starts and finishes with a row of lavender.

6 × 8 = 48 lavender bushes

7 **a** Scatter graph, histogram, bar chart, pie chart

b A scatter graph won't be appropriate because we don't have two pieces of information about the same thing.

A histogram only works for numerical data.

A bar chart would work, as would a pie chart.

c Shop A   Shop B

Tea
Americano
Espresso
Latté
Cappuccino

In shop A, tea and americanos are much more popular that the other drinks.

In shop B, lattés and cappuccinos are much more popular.

		Shop A		Shop B	
Type of drink	Frequency	Angle	Frequency	Angle
Tea	28	28 × 5 = 140	15	15 × 4 = 60
Americano	22	22 × 5 = 110	8	8 × 4 = 32
Espresso	9	9 × 5 = 45	6	6 × 4 = 24
Latté	6	6 × 5 = 30	35	35 × 4 = 140
Cappuccino	7	7 × 5 = 35	26	26 × 4 = 104
Total	72	360°	90	360°

For Shop A: 360° ÷ 72 = 5°. For Shop B: 360° ÷ 90 = 4°.

8

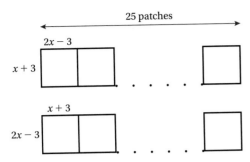

There are 25 patches in each row.

The width could be $25(x + 3) = 25x + 75$

or it could be $25(2x - 3) = 50x - 75$

a $25x + 75$ or $50x - 75$

b $64x - 96$ or $32x + 96$

$32(2x - 3)$ or $32(x + 3)$

c $64x - 96 = 64 \times 5 - 96 = 224\,\text{cm}$

$25x + 75 = 25 \times 5 + 75 = 200\,\text{cm}$

$x + 3 = 8$

$x = 5$

For the first option the dimensions are 2.24 m by 2 m.

The alternative version gives a size of 1.75 m by 2.56 m.

There may be two sets of dimensions, but the area is always the same!

9　**a** 4 metres

One less than five bricks = 4

b 4 bricks

Length + 1 = number of bricks

c

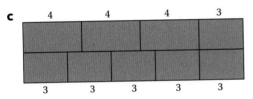

Any combination of 4 and 3 to total 15. Draw a diagram to help.

Option 1: 4 m + 4 m + 4 m + 3 m

Option 2: 3 m + 3 m + 3 m + 3 m + 3 m

d Option 1: 19 bricks

Option 2: 20 bricks

4 m + 4 m + 4 m + 3 m would need: 5 + 5 + 5 + 4 bricks (for every metre of plank there is one extra brick)

or

3 m + 3 m + 3 m + 3 m + 3 m would need: 4 + 4 + 4 + 4 + 4 bricks

10

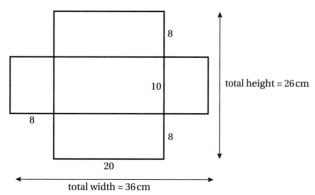

A diagram showing all the faces of the box will help.

a $20 \times 10 + 10 \times 8 \times 2 + 20 \times 8 \times 2 = 680 \,\text{cm}^2$

b

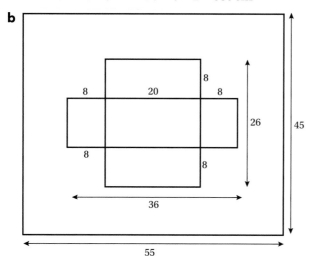

$45 - 26 = 19\,\text{cm}$, which is more than enough to go across the rim of the box and inside.

$55 - 36 = 19\,\text{cm}$, so it will work in that direction too.

The piece of paper **is** big enough.

 11

Start with a diagram to show what is going on:

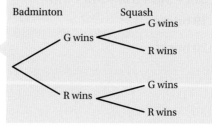

Then fill in the probabilities.

a $0.85 \times 0.35 = 0.2975$

b $0.15 \times 0.35 = 0.0525$

c $0.85 \times 0.65 + 0.15 \times 0.35 = 0.605$

12

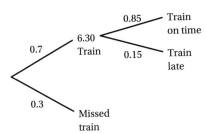

A tree diagram might be useful here.

Probability Leela is on time is $0.7 \times 0.85 = 0.595$

---

13 **a**

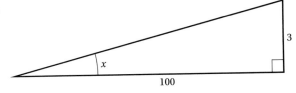

If you draw a diagram to represent the slope, you get a right-angled triangle.

Use trigonometry to calculate the angle of this slope.

$\tan x = \dfrac{3}{100}$

$x = 1.7°$ (1 dp)

b

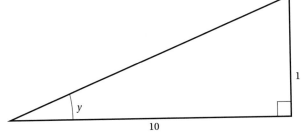

$\tan y = \dfrac{1}{10}$

$y = 5.7°$ (1 dp)

The difference between the slopes is $3.9922°$.

It is $4.0°$ steeper.

---

14 a

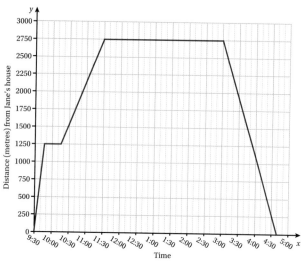

Horizontal lines indicate there is no change in the distance travelled.

b Distance travelled = 1500 m = 1.5 km

Time taken = 10.15 to 11.30, which is $1\frac{1}{4}$ hours.

Speed = $1.5 \div 1\frac{1}{4}$ = 1.2 km/h

$$\text{Speed} = \frac{\text{distance}}{\text{time}}$$

c Distance = 2750 m = 2.75 km

Time = 1 h 40 min = $1 + \frac{40}{60}$ hour = $1\frac{2}{3}$ h

Speed = $2750 \div 1\frac{2}{3}$

= 1.65 km/h

15 a

The graph is helpful in answering the rest of this question.

b Wheelies Rental

c £5

Whacky Wheels: £35 + £75 = £110
Wheelie Rentals: 500 × £0.23 = £115

16

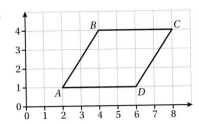

A diagram of the situation helps you see what is going on.

a $\overrightarrow{CD} = \begin{pmatrix} -2 \\ -3 \end{pmatrix}$

b $\overrightarrow{AB} = \begin{pmatrix} 2 \\ 3 \end{pmatrix}$

The length AB is the same as the length CD but the vectors are in opposite directions.

c ABCD is a parallelogram: a four-sided shape with two sets of parallel sides.

BC is $\begin{pmatrix} 4 \\ 0 \end{pmatrix}$ and AD is $\begin{pmatrix} 4 \\ 0 \end{pmatrix}$ so BC is parallel to AD.

AB is $\begin{pmatrix} 2 \\ 3 \end{pmatrix}$ and DC is $\begin{pmatrix} 2 \\ 3 \end{pmatrix}$ so AB is parallel to DC.

17 The diameter of the cherry tree is 3 m. Assume it has a radius of 1.5 m. This means the tree can be planted anywhere 1.5 m away from the edge of the lawn.

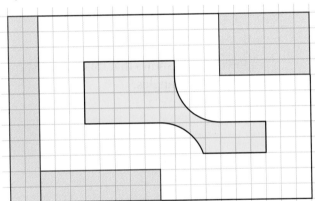

This diagram has a scale of two squares to 1 m. The yellow area is where the cherry tree can be planted.

You can choose any scale you like.

To show where the cherry tree can go there are straight lines 1.5 m away from the edge of the lawn and arcs (parts of circles) at the corners of the flower bed and the vegetable patch.

The helicopters cover 25 km from each town, so you need two circles. The fire brigade covers the section closer to B than A, so you need the locus of points equidistant from both towns.

Scale: 1 cm represents 5 km

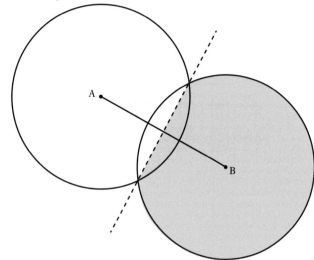

This diagram uses a scale of 1 cm = 5 km (you might have chosen a different scale).

Start with a line of 8 cm (to represent the 40 km distance between the towns).

With compasses draw a circle centre B and radius 5 cm.

With compasses draw a circle centre A and radius 5 cm.

The locus of points equidistant from B and A is the perpendicular bisector of line AB.

Shade the region that is closer to B than A and covered by helicopter B.

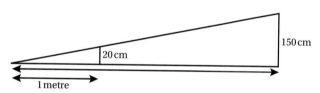

A good diagram shows that this is a question about similar triangles.

The scale factor of the enlargement is

150 cm ÷ 20 cm = 7.5

1 m × 7.5 = 7.5 m

The image needs to be 7.5 times larger to fill the screen. This means that the projector needs to be 7.5 times further away.

20 **a i, ii**

There are three possible triangles that fit Harriet's description.

iii She could say that the hypotenuse is 5 cm.

For only one triangle to be possible, Harriet must make sure that her conditions follow one of the conditions of congruence:

SSS, SAS, ASA, AAS or RHS

b i

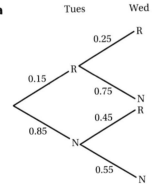

There is only one triangle that satisfies Janet's conditions because she has given SAS.

ii A scale drawing will enable you to measure the length of the third side as 5.7 cm to the nearest mm.

21 **a**

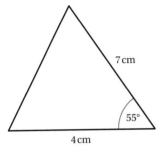

Key

R = rain

N = no rain

A tree diagram is often helpful in probability questions.

b $0.15 \times 0.25 = 0.0375$

c $(0.15 \times 0.75) + (0.85 \times 0.45) = 0.495$

22 a

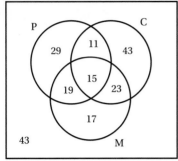

200 students

Let studying Chemistry be event C.

Let studying Physics be event P.

Let studying Maths be event M.

b $\dfrac{17}{200}$

c $\dfrac{68}{200} = \dfrac{17}{50}$

$11 + 19 + 23 + 15 = 68$

23 a

A graph showing the lengths they have swum might be helpful.

The line for Caroline's graph is always below Janet's so there is no time when Caroline has swum further than Janet.

b 20 minutes

c $\dfrac{45}{30} = 1.5$ lengths per minute

24 a

b

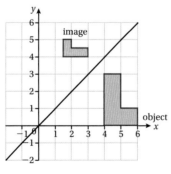

Choose a shape without any symmetry to easily see what is going on.

The orientation and size of the final image are the same when the transformations are carried out in a different order, but it ends up in a different place.

1 $\sqrt{64} = 8$

> You can't tell immediately, but it seems sensible to work out $\sqrt{64}$.

$10\sqrt{64} = 10 \times 8 = 80$

$10\sqrt{64} = 80$ so the statement $(10\sqrt{64} < 80)$ is false.

---

2 $5 \times 12 = 60$

> If the mean of 5 numbers is 12, what do you know? When you work out the mean of five numbers you add them up and divide by 5, so before the sum was divided by 5 it must have totalled 60 (because $60 \div 5 = 12$).

$x + x + 3x + 4x + 6x = 60$

> Use the ratios to form an equation.

$$15x = 60$$
$$x = \frac{60}{15} = 4$$

The largest number is $6 \times 4 = 24$

3

45°

> Because of the way the paper has been folded you know the marked angle is 45°.

$360° \div 45° = 8$, so 8 of the kites will fit together.

---

4 A sleeper is 8.5 feet long.

$8.5 \times 30 = 255 \, \text{cm} = 2.55 \, \text{m}$

> It is sensible to first convert the length of a sleeper to centimetres.
>
> An alternative would be to convert the length of the border into feet.

$\dfrac{20 \, \text{m}}{2.55 \, \text{m}} = 7.8...$, which means he needs 8 sleepers

It will cost him $8 \times £22 = £176$

---

5 $2 \times (6 \, \text{m} + 4 \, \text{m}) = 20 \, \text{m}$

> You can't work out the cost, but you can work out the perimeter of the living room.

$85 \, \text{cm} \div 100 = 0.85 \, \text{m}$

> Convert the width of a door to metres.

$20 - 2 \times 0.85 = 18.3 \, \text{m}$

It looks as though he needs to buy whole metres of skirting board, so 19 m is needed.

> Subtract the width of the two doors from the perimeter.

$£4.31 \times 19 = £81.89$

6 **a** 3 : 5 gives 8 parts.

32 ÷ 8 = 4

There are 3 × 4 = 12 non-calculator questions in each test.

b There are 5 × 4 = 20 calculator questions in each test.

15 tests × 20 = 300 calculator questions

c 15 × 32 = 480 questions, so each teacher will write 240 questions.

Miss Smith will write 15 × 12 = 180 non-calculator questions, so she will have to write 240 – 180 = 60 calculator questions.

d $\dfrac{60}{240} = \dfrac{1}{4}$

> Start by working out the number of parts in the ratio.

> This is complicated, so let's find out how many questions there are altogether.

---

7 **a**

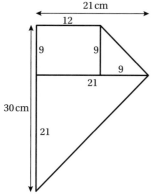

Rectangle: 12 × 9 = 108

Small triangle: $\dfrac{1}{2}$ × 9 × 9 = 40.5

Large triangle: $\dfrac{1}{2}$ × 21 × 21 = 220.5

Total area = 369 cm²

b Area of the original sheet is 21 × 30 = 630 cm²

The fraction is $\dfrac{369}{630} = \dfrac{41}{70}$

> Draw a good diagram and then work out the lengths of the sides.

> The two right-angled triangles are each half a square and this helps you to work out the lengths.

> Now there is enough information to work out the areas.

> Either work out the area of the rectangle and the two triangles and add them, or work out the area of the original sheet of paper and subtract two triangles.

8 The perimeters are quite difficult to work out because of the diagonal lines involved, so it doesn't look likely that the perimeters are involved.

> Maybe this is something to do with the perimeters of the shapes.

Some of the shapes have symmetry:

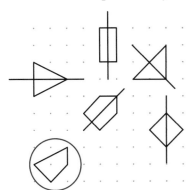

> Perhaps it is a symmetry problem. Try checking the symmetry of the shapes.

There is only one that does not have any lines of symmetry, so this could be the odd one out.

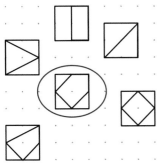

> Perhaps the difference has to do with the areas of the shapes.
>
> To work out the areas, you could draw a 2 by 2 square around each shape.

The shape that is circled is the only one that has an area that is not half of the square, so this could be the odd one out.

9

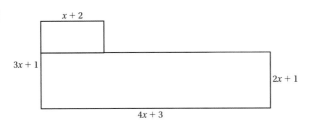

> You can't work out the area of the whole shape at the moment, but you can work out the area of the rectangles. There are several ways to divide up the shape. The diagram shows one.

a The area is $x(x + 2) + (2x + 1)(4x + 3)$

$= 9x^2 + 12x + 3$

b $x = \dfrac{(16 - 1)}{3} = 5$

c Area $= 9 \times 5^2 + 12 \times 5 + 3 = 288\,\text{m}^2$

d The perimeter $= 14x + 8$. When $x = 5$ the perimeter is $14 \times 5 + 8 = 78\,\text{m}$. The posts are 1 m apart so 78 posts will be needed.

e $78 \times 3 = 234\,\text{m}$ of wire.

f $78 \times 18.5 + 234 \times 2.30 = £1981.20$

A	7.	Total number of sixes is 7.
		Relative frequency is 0.7.
B	4.	Total number of sixes is 11 out of 20.
		Relative frequency is 0.55.
C	3.	Total number of sixes is 14.
		Relative frequency is 0.47.
D	6.	Total number of sixes is 20.
		Relative frequency is 0.5.
E	4.	Total number of sixes is 24.
		Relative frequency is 0.48.

It probably (!) makes sense to start working out the probability after each child has had a go.

After 10 children have done their throws there are 44 sixes and the relative frequency is 0.44.

Now you might want to skip a few.

After 15 children have done their throws there are 68 sixes and the relative frequency is 0.45.

After 20 children have done their throws there are 83 sixes and the relative frequency is 0.415.

The relative frequency is going up and down, but it looks as if it is settling somewhere close to 0.4.

When more trials happen the relative frequency is generally closer to the actual value, so the actual value of the probability is probably about 0.4, which means that the dice is a biased one.

$300\,000\,000 \div 10 = 30\,000\,000$ miles in one year

$30\,000\,000 \div 365 = 82\,191.78$ miles in one day

$82\,191.78 \div 24 = 3424.6575$ miles per hour

Start by working out what you can.

You need to assume that the probe travels at a constant speed.

The probe travelled 300 000 000 miles in 10 years. Work out how many miles it travelled per hour.

$3424.6575 \div 290 = 11.8$

The probe travels about 12 times as fast as the car.

Divide this by 290.

An alternative method would be to work out how far the car would travel in 10 years.

Volume of cylinder $= \pi \times 3^2 \times 11 = 311.01767... \text{ cm}^3$

$= 311 \text{ cm}^3$ (3 sf)

You could start by working out the volume of a cylinder of water that is 11 cm high.

Volume of water (a cylinder) = area of circular base × height

$311 \text{ cm}^3 = 311 \text{ ml}$

Write the volume of water in ml.

Volume of water left in bottle = 500 ml − 311 ml

$= 189 \text{ ml}$ (3 sf)

13 $4 \times 4 \times 4 = 64 \, \text{cm}^3$

Two cubes have a volume of $128 \, \text{cm}^3$.

If h is the increase in the height of the water, the volume of the extra water is: $\pi r^2 h$

The radius of the tube is 4 cm, so:

$\pi \times 4^2 \times h = 128$

$16\pi \times h = 128$

$h = \dfrac{128}{16\pi}$

$h = 2.5 \, \text{cm} \, (1 \, \text{dp})$

> Work out the volume of a steel cube.

> This means you know what the extra volume is.

> When two cubes are dropped into the cylinder, the water level goes up. The increase in water volume is the same as the volume of the cubes.

14 **a**

The area of the triangular cross-section is
$\dfrac{1}{2} \times 6 \times 8 = 24 \, \text{cm}^2$

The volume of the prism is $24 \times 9 = 216 \, \text{cm}^3$

b The volume of the pentagonal prism is
$36 \times L = 216 \, \text{cm}^3$

$L = 216 \div 36 = 6 \, \text{cm}$

> First, label a copy of the diagram.

> Now you can work out the volume of the triangular prism.

> That helps you work out the length of the pentagonal prism.

15 **a** $7 \times £4.20 = £29.80$

If each friend pays $£x$, then $6x + 20 \geqslant 29.80$

b $6x + 20 \geqslant 29.80$ means that $x \geqslant 1.633333 \ldots$

They must bring at least £1.64 each.

> Start with the total cost of the equipment.

> (It will be higher than this because you don't know how much the drinks and snacks will cost.)

> There are six friends and they will each pay the same amount. Daniel has £20.

16

| A | 3 cm | B | | C | | D | area = 24 cm² |

2 cm   area = 12 cm²   perimeter = 20 cm   4 cm

A and D are similar because the lengths of the sides of D are twice those of A.

We cannot tell whether B or C are also similar.

> Start by drawing all the shapes.

> You know all about A.
>
> B could have lots of different dimensions (1 × 12, 3 × 4, 8 × 1.5, and so on). C could have lots of different dimensions (2 × 8, 1.5 × 8.5, and so on).
>
> D has a length of 4 cm and must have a height of 6 cm.

17

a $40 \times 30 = 1200$ unit squares

$\frac{4}{5}$ of 1200 = 960

You want to have $\frac{5}{6}$ of 1200 = 1000 shaded, so you need to shade an extra 40 unit squares.

b 960 is shaded from the first rectangle.

$\frac{2}{3}$ of 1200 = 800 is shaded from the second rectangle.

The fraction of the whole thing that is shaded is:

$$\frac{960 + 800}{1200 + 1200} = \frac{1760}{2400} = \frac{11}{15}$$

c $\frac{3}{4}$ of 2400 = 1800, so an extra 40 unit squares need to be shaded.

> You could start by working out the area of the rectangle.

> Now you can work out the shaded area.

> You already know that 1760 unit squares are shaded.

18 **a** The angles in a regular hexagon are 120°, and those in a regular pentagon are 108°.

The angles around a point should add up to 360°, but here they total 120° + 216° = 336°, pentagons cannot be used to fit round the hexagon.

b 3 × 120° = 360°, so regular hexagons will fit around the edge. Equilateral triangles would also fit:

c A regular decagon can be surrounded by regular pentagons.

Two regular pentagons have angles of

108°+ 108° = 216°.

This leaves 360° – 216° = 144°,

which is the interior angle of a regular decagon.

The interior angle of a regular pentagon is 108°.

You have to identify the regular polygon that has an interior angle of 144°.

The exterior angle is 180° – 144° = 36°

Exterior angles always sum to 360°, so there must be 10 of them and the shape must have 10 sides.

a $4x + 6y = 9.20$

> Let x be the cost of a cup of tea and y be the cost of a cupcake.

b $5x + 2y = 7.10$

c $4x + 6y = 9.20$

$5x + 2y = 7.10$

$15x + 6y = 21.30$ (multiply the second equation by 3)

$11x = 12.10$ (subtract the first equation from the third)

> Solve for x.

$x = 1.10$ (a cup of tea costs £1.10)

> Substitute for x in the first equation.

$4 \times 1.10 + 6y = 9.20$

$6y = 4.80$

> Solve for y.

$y = 0.80$ (a cupcake costs £0.80)

 a $220\,\text{cm} = \pi \times d$

> Circumference $= \pi \times$ diameter d

$d = 220\,\text{cm} \div \pi = 70.028\,17\ldots\,\text{cm}$

> Use inverse operations to find the value of d.

Javed's tyre has a diameter of 70 cm

b $50 \times 220\,\text{cm} = 11\,000\,\text{cm} = 110\,\text{m}$

> When the wheels go round once the bicycle will travel the length of the circumference.

c $600\,\text{m} + 550\,\text{m} + 900\,\text{m} + 550\,\text{m} + 200\,\text{m} + 350\,\text{m} + 270\,\text{m} + 150\,\text{m} + 170\,\text{m} + 200\,\text{m} = 3940\,\text{m}$

> Calculate the missing lengths on the diagram.

$3940\,\text{m} \div 2.2\,\text{m} = 1790.909\,09\ldots$

Number of revolutions $= 1791$

> This is the number of revolutions to the nearest whole number.

1 **a**

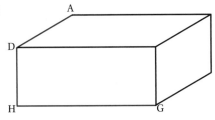

$5 + 6 + 20 = 31$ cm

Adding the ant's route to a copy of the diagram might help.

b

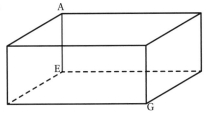

There are several different ways to go via E. The quickest ones still involve using 5, 6 and 20 = 31 cm

c

The smallest route is around the smallest rectangle:

$5 + 6 + 5 + 6 = 22$ cm

d

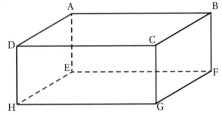

B→A→D→C→G→H→E→F→B gives a length of 102 cm

It is not possible to go along every edge, so use the longest edges as much as possible.

2 **a**

The extra lines on the diagram show that you need 180° plus a third of 180° (60°), which is 240° in total.

> Draw the angle you need to work out. Then a couple of extra lines will make the calculations easier.

b When the minute hand makes a full turn the hour hand moves one hour, which means the hour hand moves at $\frac{1}{12}$ of the speed.

$\frac{1}{12}$ of 240° = 20°

3

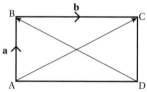

Using the algebra: $\overrightarrow{AC} = \mathbf{a} + \mathbf{b}$

$\overrightarrow{DB} = \mathbf{a} - \mathbf{b}$

Although the diagonals of the rectangle are equal in length, the vectors are going in different directions.

> Draw in the two vectors. It makes it easier to see what you are being asked.

4 **a**

The length of the fence is:

$\pi \times 17 = 53.407\,075 \ldots$ m

53.4 m

A copy of the diagram with the extra line added will help.

Circumference of circle = $\pi \times$ diameter

Round the answer to 3 sf.

b

semi circle with diameter of 10 m

Length of fence:

21.5 + 10 + 21.5 + semicircle with diameter of 10 m

Semicircle:

$\pi \times 10 \div 2 = 15.70796 \ldots$ m $= 15.7$ m (3 sf)

Total length is 53 m + 15.7 m = 68.7 m

68.7 m – 53.4 m = 15.3 m

Ian will need to buy 15.3 m more fencing than Gerry.

Calculate the difference in lengths of fencing.

Conclusion.

5

The total length is $x + x - 60 + x - 120$, which is $3x - 180$.

This is equal to 5.1 m, which is 510 cm.

$3x - 180 = 510$

$3x = 690$

$x = 230$

Sections are 230 cm, 170 cm and 110 cm.

Draw a diagram of the three sections of the ladder, with the numbers in cm.

You are told that the total length is equal to 5.1 m.

Form an equation and solve for x.

117

6

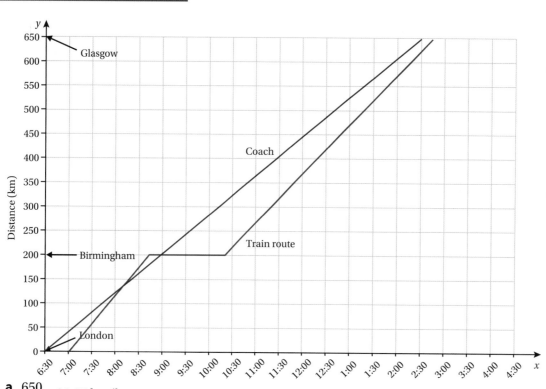

Even though you are not told to, it is helpful to draw the graphs.

Note that the graphs show 'average speeds' as the speeds will vary during the journeys.

a $\dfrac{650}{8} = 81.25$ km/h

b 1 h 40 min + 1 h 45 min + 4 h 15 min =

7 h 40 min = $7\dfrac{2}{3}$ hours

$650 \div 7\dfrac{2}{3} = 84.8$ km/h

First calculate the total time for the train journey and then convert the time to hours.

7 Length of AB = 2

Length of EF = 1

Scale factor = $\dfrac{1}{2}$

Length of BC = 6

Length of FG = $\dfrac{1}{2} \times 6 = 3$

Read off the lengths AB and EF.

Calculate the scale factor of ABCD to EFGH.

Use the scale factor to calculate the length FG (corresponding to BC).

Drawing this onto a copy of the diagram will help.

G: (1.5, 2.5) and H: (0.5, 2.5)

8 Left-hand triangle:

180 − (30 + 90) = 60°

Right-hand triangle:

180 − (60 + 90) = 30°

The two triangles are identical because they are congruent, by ASA. Therefore they have the same area.

This time the useful idea is actually to find the missing angles of the triangles.

Use the fact that angles in a triangle sum to 180°.

This means they must have the same area and you don't need to work out the two areas (which are 36.6 mm² (3 sf)).

---

9 a

Congruent shapes have the same area, so you could start by working out the area of the original diagram, which is 12 square units.

To have three congruent shapes the area of each one must be 4 square units. An easy way to make an area of 4 is to have a square.

b

To make four congruent shapes the area of each one must be 3 square units. If you try to use three straight lines it doesn't work, either with rectangles or with triangles. There are other shapes that have an area of 3 square units, and these will work here.

10

First you could draw extra lines on the diagram to work out the answer.

$\frac{9}{16}$ of the diagram is purple.

Team A have given an area rather than a proportion.
0 marks

Team B have got the wrong fraction. Maybe they saw that $\frac{3}{4}$ of this part was shaded:

But that is not the whole thing. 0 or 1 mark

Team C are correct. Maybe they used the idea that the inner big white triangle is not included (leaving $\frac{3}{4}$ of the whole diagram) and then $\frac{3}{4}$ of that is shaded, which is $\frac{3}{4} \times \frac{3}{4}$. This equals $\frac{9}{16}$. 4 marks

Team D are correct. $\frac{9}{16} = 0.5625$. 4 marks

11 **a**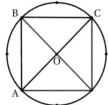

The inner shape is a square, so the angle ABC is 90°

> Here are some extra lines that make it easier to see what is going on.

b

> The extra lines show that there are 8 equal angles around the centre of the circle.
>
> Each angle is therefore 360° ÷ 8 = 45°.

> Triangle OCB is isosceles, which means angles B and C are equal and add up to 135°. Each one is therefore 67.5°.

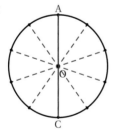

> Triangle OAB is also isosceles and the angle AOB = 135° (three lots of 45°). Angles A and B are equal and add up to 45°, so each one is 22.5°.

Angle ABC is 67.5° + 22.5° = 90°

c

The angles around the centre are all 36° (360° ÷ 10). When you choose a point for B you will make isosceles triangles and can work out the other angles as in part **b**.

12   Area of the classic pizza = $\pi \times 6^2$

$$= 113.0973 \ldots \text{ inches}^2$$

The area of the rustic pizza is a rectangle of 7×11 plus a circle (two semi circles) of radius 3.5 inches.

11 inches

7 inches

18 inches

Area = $7 \times 11 + \pi \times 3.5^2$

$$= 115.4845 \ldots \text{ inches}^2$$

You do get a little more for your money when you buy the rustic pizza. The area is approximately 2 inches^2 larger than the classic pizza.

> Work out the area of the classic pizza.

> Work out the area of the rustic pizza.

> The extra lines show that it is a rectangle with two semi circles.

> Conclusion.

13

> This is a hard question. A well-labelled diagram might help.

> In this triangle the marked angle is 60° and the length of BC is 2. Use trigonometry to work out that the horizontal distance is $2 \times \sin 60° = \sqrt{3}$ and that the vertical distance is $2 \times \cos 60° = 1$.

a $\overrightarrow{DE}$ is the same vector as $\overrightarrow{BA}$. This is $\begin{pmatrix} 0 \\ -2 \end{pmatrix}$

> The same numbers as $\overrightarrow{AB}$ but with the opposite sign.

b $\overrightarrow{BC} = \begin{pmatrix} \sqrt{3} \\ 1 \end{pmatrix}$

> To get from B to C you need to go right by $\sqrt{3}$ and up by 1.

c   The vector $\overrightarrow{FC} = \begin{pmatrix} 0 \\ 4 \end{pmatrix}$

> F is immediately below C. C is 1 above B, so F must be 1 below A, which means the distance from F to C is 4.

d $\overrightarrow{AE} = \begin{pmatrix} 2\sqrt{3} \\ 0 \end{pmatrix}$

> The vector $\overrightarrow{AE}$ is the same as the vector $\overrightarrow{BD}$. D is level with B, so you just need to look at how far D is to the right of B. To get from B to C you go right by $\sqrt{3}$, so you need to double this.

e $\overrightarrow{AC} = \begin{pmatrix} 0 \\ 2 \end{pmatrix} + \begin{pmatrix} \sqrt{3} \\ 1 \end{pmatrix} = \begin{pmatrix} \sqrt{3} \\ 3 \end{pmatrix}$

> The vector $\overrightarrow{AC}$ is the same as $\overrightarrow{AB} + \overrightarrow{BC}$.

f $\overrightarrow{EF}$ is the same vector as $\overrightarrow{CB}$. This is $\begin{pmatrix} -\sqrt{3} \\ 1 \end{pmatrix}$

> The same numbers as $\overrightarrow{BC}$ but with the opposite sign.

a 3.6 m = 360 cm

360 cm ÷ 18 cm = 20 stairs in the staircase.

> The stairs must cover a vertical distance of 3.6 m. Each step is 18 cm high.

b Base length of staircase = 20 × 28 cm = 560 cm

> The banister rail will go diagonally up the stairs. It will need to be the same length as the diagonal length of the staircase. Use Pythagoras' theorem to calculate this.

$a^2 + b^2 = c^2$

$560^2 + 360^2 = c^2$

$443\,200 = c^2$

$c = 665.73... \text{ cm}$

The banister rail will need to be 6.66 m in length (to the nearest cm).

---

 a

> If they are looking up at an angle of 45°, then they create a right-angled, isosceles triangle. (The triangle is isosceles because if one angle is 90° and another is 45° then the remaining angle will also be 45°.)

> Draw the extra lines on the diagram so that you can see what is going on.

Assuming that the child's height is small compared to the height of the tree, then the horizontal distance along the ground is approximately the same as the height of the tree (two equal sides in an isosceles triangle).

b

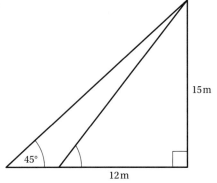

> A good diagram will help.

Opposite side = height of tree = 15 m

Adjacent side = 12 m

Guy's angle = $\tan^{-1} \dfrac{15}{12} = 51.34 \ldots °$

Guy's angle is approximately 51°.

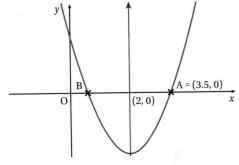

The coordinates of point B are (0.5, 0).

C is (3.5, 0) and D is (0.5, 0).

The question says that the graph is symmetrical about the line $x = 2$, so it makes sense to draw that line in.

Now you can see that the crossing value for point A is 1.5 to the right of the line of reflection, so point B must cross at 1.5 to the left of the line.

In the second diagram the quadratic has been reflected in the x-axis so the crossing points are the same.

1 **a** $1 \times 7, 2 \times 7, 3 \times 7, 4 \times 7, 5 \times 7, 6 \times 7 \dots$

    7,   14,   21,   28,   35,   42   …

$35 - 10 = 25$

Jamie's initial number was 5.

> To solve a simpler problem think about just multiplying by 7: forget about subtracting 10, at least initially. So inspect multiples of 7.

> Now think about subtracting 10.

> $5 \times 7 = 35$

> This simplification allows us to see inside the problem. Now move to a more efficient approach.

Let Jamie's number be x.

$7x - 10 = 25$

$7x = 25 + 10$

$7x = 35$ so $x = 5$

b $1 \times 4, 2 \times 4, 3 \times 4, 4 \times 4, 5 \times 4, 6 \times 4 \dots$

    4,   8,   12,   16,   **20**,   24   …

$11 + 9 = 20$

> Simon's final answer is 5. To solve a simpler problem think about multiples of 4.

> Now think about what needs to be added to 9 to make 20.

Simon's initial number was 11.

Let Simon's number be y.

$\dfrac{(y + 9)}{4} = 5$

$y + 9 = 20$

$y = 20 - 9 = 11$

> Now move to a more efficient approach.

2

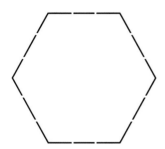

> You could start by drawing a diagram.

> You can see that there are 18 panels and that the total perimeter is 10.8 m.

Each panel is $10.8 \div 18 = 0.6$ m.

---

3 A box like this:

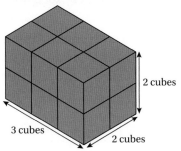

To start with, ignore the measurements on the cubes.

will hold $2 \times 2 \times 3 = 12$ cubes.

So you need three numbers that multiply together to make 40.

a, b There are several ways of packing the cubes, which include:

$4 \times 2 \times 5$ (8 (4×2) cubes in each of 5 layers)

$5 \times 2 \times 4$ (10 (5×2) cubes in each of 4 layers)

$8 \times 1 \times 5$ (8 (8×1) cubes in each of 5 layers)

$2 \times 2 \times 10$ (4 (2×2) cubes in each of 10 layers)

The first of these looks like this:

4 **a** Percentage decrease $= \dfrac{0.60}{7.60}$

$= 7.89\%$

> The discount on each adult ticket is £0.60.

> Because the cinema is assumed to be full on both days you don't need to work out the total for 150 people but can just compare the cost of a single seat.

b Percentage decrease $= \dfrac{0.45}{3.40}$

$= 13.2\%$

> The discount on each child ticket is £0.45.

c £7.60 + £3.40 = £11.00

> There are the same number of adults as children, so work out the cost of 1 adult and 1 child ticket on a normal day.

£7.00 + £2.95 = £9.95

> Work out the cost of 1 adult and 1 child ticket on a Thursday.

$\dfrac{1.05}{11.00} = 9.55\%$

> Work out the percentage loss.

 5 Even + even = even

Odd + odd = even

Even + odd = odd

> Think about what happens when you add odd and even numbers.

Even × even = even

Odd × odd = odd

Even × even × even... = even

Odd × odd × odd... = odd

> Then do the same for multiplication:

a $4^3 = 4 \times 4 \times 4$ is even

$3^4 = 3 \times 3 \times 3 \times 3$ is odd

Even + odd is odd

So $4^3 + 3^4$ is odd

> An even number raised to any whole-number power is even:
>
> $(\text{even})^x = \text{even}$

b 6^7 is even

3^7 is odd

So $6^7 + 3^7$ is odd

> An odd number raised to any whole-number power is odd:
>
> $(\text{odd})^x = \text{odd}$

6 **a** The diagram shows two wedges. That means 20 of these pairs total a metre long, so *x* must be 5 cm.

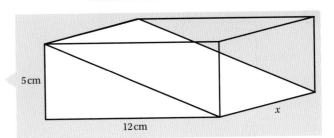

5 cm

12 cm

x

b To make £30 profit and cover the cost of the wood (£5), Ahmed has to take at least £35.

As he has 40 wedges to sell, the minimum cost to achieve this is £35 ÷ 40 = 87.5p for each wedge.

This rounds to 88p.

7 Probability Helen does not have to stop =

$\frac{9}{10} \times \frac{3}{4} \times \frac{1}{3} = \frac{27}{120}$

Probability Helen has to stop at least once =

$1 - \frac{27}{120} = \frac{93}{120}$

This simplifies to $\frac{31}{40}$

A simpler problem would be to work out the probability she doesn't have to stop.

You can then work out the probability she does have to stop at least once.

8 **a, c**

An accurate graph makes the question easy.

b £27

d 4 hours

127

9

Make this simpler by focusing on the right-angled triangle first.

Use Pythagoras' theorem to work out the base of this triangle.

$\sqrt{22^2 - 20^2} = \sqrt{84} = 9.165...$

The distance across the top of the trapezium is therefore $30 - 9.165 = 20.8\,\text{mm}$ (3 sf).

10

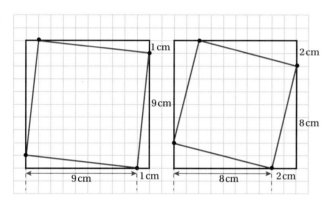

Label what you know. Use the squares on the paper to find the lengths.

$a^2 + b^2 = c^2$ $a^2 + b^2 = c^2$

$9^2 + 1^2 = c^2$ $8^2 + 2^2 = c^2$

$82 = c^2$ $68 = c^2$

$c = \sqrt{82} = 9.055...\,\text{cm}$ $c = \sqrt{68} = 8.246...\,\text{cm}$

Now focus on a triangle. Use Pythagoras' theorem to calculate the side length of the titled square.

A line in the first logo is longer than a line in the second logo, so the total line length of the first logo is greater.

11 $1\,000\,000 \div 60 = 16\,666.666\ldots$ minutes

$16\,666.666\ldots \div 60 = 277.777\ldots$ hours

$277.777\ldots \div 24 = 11.574$ days

If each number takes about 2 seconds to say (on average), then it will take about 23 days to say them all.

Even allowing for breaks for sleeping and eating, you could easily do this in your lifetime.

> This method starts by working out how many days is the same as 1 million seconds

> Some numbers will be much quicker to say than others. It is quick to say 'three' or 'five hundred thousand', but it takes much longer to say 'two hundred and twenty-two thousand, two hundred and twenty-two'.

12 a Principal $\times 1.08^{10}$

= Principal $\times 2.16$

Yes, he would more than double his money.

b $£40\,000 \times 1.08^{10}$

= $£86\,357$ to the nearest pound

c $£30\,000 \times 1.08^{10} = £64\,767.75$

$£31\,000 \times 1.08^{10} = £66\,926.67$

$£32\,000 \times 1.08^{10} = £69\,085.60$

$£33\,000 \times 1.08^{10} = £71\,244.52$

$£34\,000 \times 1.08^{10} = £73\,403.45$

$£35\,000 \times 1.08^{10} = £75\,562.37$

The smallest amount that Larry's aunt must invest is $£35\,000$.

> 8% interest is an increase with a multiplier of 1.08.

> The bank only gives this deal for $£30\,000$ or more so start checking from this amount.

> Another way to work it out is to divide $£75\,000$ by 1.08^{10}.

13

The two semi circles make a circle, radius 2.25 cm.

Area of circle $= \pi \times 2.25^2 = 15.9043\ldots$ cm^2

Height of triangle $= 13 - 2.25 = 10.75$ cm

Area of triangle $= \frac{1}{2} \times 9 \times 10.75 = 48.375$ cm^2

$9 \times 13 - 15.9043 - 48.375 = 52.7$ cm^2 (3 sf)

> Start by working out the areas of the different parts of the heart.

> Subtract the areas of the circle and triangle from the area of the rectangle.

14

a $140 \div 1\frac{1}{2} = 93.3 \, \text{km/h}$

b $140 \div 1\frac{1}{3} = 105 \, \text{km/h}$

c 10 minutes

d 12 noon

e 4.5 hours, $\dfrac{280}{4.5} = 62.2 \, \text{km/h}$

f 3 hours 40 minutes, $\dfrac{280}{3.666} = 76.4 \, \text{km/h}$

g 105 km/h is only 65.6 miles per hour, so neither of them was speeding at any point as long as the speed limit was 70 mph.

Read the graph to work out the times: Dave takes 1h 30 min to travel 140 km; Hazel takes 1 h 20 min to travel the first stage of her journey.

1 **a** Both answers are the same, $1\frac{1}{3}$

Only the order in which they are added is different.

b $1 - \frac{1}{3} = \frac{2}{3}$ but $\frac{1}{3} - 1 = -\frac{2}{3}$

The only difference between the two subtraction answers is the negative symbol.

2 **i** You could:
- multiply $\frac{1}{4}$ by anything bigger than 2
- divide $\frac{1}{4}$ by anything between 0 and $\frac{1}{2}$
- add anything bigger than $\frac{1}{4}$ or subtract anything less than $\frac{(-1)}{4}$ to $\frac{1}{4}$.

3 **a** e.g. $\frac{1}{50}, \frac{1}{49}, \frac{1}{48}, \frac{1}{47}, \frac{1}{46}$

b e.g. $\frac{2}{6}, \frac{2}{5}, \frac{2}{4}, \frac{2}{3}, \frac{2}{2}$

c e.g. $\frac{6}{2}, \frac{7}{2}, \frac{8}{2}, \frac{9}{2}, \frac{10}{2}$

or

$\frac{5}{3}, \frac{7}{4}, \frac{9}{5}, \frac{8}{3}, \frac{9}{2}$

4 To 1 significant figure this calculation is $20 \times 800 = 16\,000$, which is about 10 times the size of 1903.02. The answer is likely to be incorrect.

Start with $23.64 \times 805 = 1903.02$

If $23.64 \times 805 = 1903.02$ is true, then:

$2.364 \times 805 = 190.302$

and $2.364 \times 8.05 = 1.90302$

The left-hand side must be bigger than 16, so the calculation can't be correct.

5 **a** $1 - (0.2 + 0.7) = 0.1$

b $0.7 \times 140 = 98$

c The number of bulbs that grow =

$\dfrac{6}{7} \times 140 = 120$

The number of those bulbs that are red =

$\dfrac{1}{5} \times 120 = 24$

> Change $\dfrac{1}{5}$ into 0.2

---

6 **a** $400\,\text{mg} = 0.4\,\text{g}$

$400\,\text{g} + 400\,\text{mg} = 400.4\,\text{g}$

$0.5\,\text{kg} = 500\,\text{g}$

$0.5\,\text{kg} - 90\,\text{g} = 410\,\text{g}$

$400\,\text{g} + 400\,\text{mg} < 0.5\,\text{kg} - 90\,\text{g}$

> Change the quantities so they use the same units. It makes sense to work in grams. $1\,\text{kg} = 1000\,\text{g}$ and $1\,\text{g} = 1000\,\text{mg}$

b $0.1\,\text{km} = 100\,\text{m}$

$150\,\text{cm} = 1.5\,\text{m}$

$0.1\,\text{km} + 150\,\text{cm} = 101.5\,\text{m}$

$900\,\text{cm} = 9\,\text{m}$

$110\,\text{m} - 900\,\text{cm} = 101\,\text{m}$

$0.1\,\text{km} + 150\,\text{cm} > 110\,\text{m} - 900\,\text{cm}$

> Convert everything to metres. $1\,\text{km} = 1000\,\text{m}$ and $1\,\text{m} = 100\,\text{cm}$

c 0.75 hours = 45 minutes

600 seconds = 10 minutes

0.75 hours + 600 seconds = 55 minutes

0.1 hours = 6 minutes

50 minutes + 0.1 hours = 56 minutes

0.75 hours + 600 seconds < 50 minutes + 0.1 hours

> Convert everything to minutes.

7

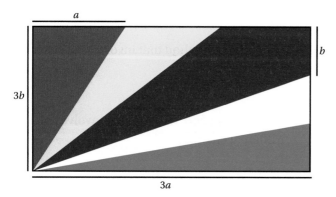

> Label the triangles.
>
> Across the top of the flag each triangle has a side that is a, which means the whole flag has a width of $3a$. On the right, each triangle has a side that is b, which means the whole flag has a height of $3b$.

The area of the white triangle is $\dfrac{1}{2} \times b \times 3a = \dfrac{1}{2} \times 3ab$

The area of the blue triangle is $\dfrac{1}{2} \times a \times 3b = \dfrac{1}{2} \times 3ab$

This shows that the two areas are the same.

> Now use the formula for the area of a triangle.

8 Snail 1:   36 000 mm/h ($\div$ 10)

3600 cm/h ($\div$ 60)

60 cm/min ($\div$ 60)

1 cm/s

Snail 2:   0.01 m/s ($\times$ 100)

1 cm/s

Snail 3:   5 km/day ($\times$ 1000)

5000 m/day ($\times$ 100)

500 000 cm/day ($\div$ 24)

20 833.333... cm/h ($\div$ 60)

347.222... cm/min ($\div$ 60)

5.787... cm/s (= 5.8 cm/s to 1 dp)

Snail 4:   700 cm/h ($\div$ 60)

11.666... cm/min ($\div$ 60)

0.19444... cm/s (= 0.2 cm/s to 1 dp)

Snail 3 finishes first.

> To compare the snails' speeds they must be measured in the same units.
>
> In this question it might be sensible to convert all the speeds into cm per second (cm/s).

---

9 **a** $1 + 2 + 3 = 6$, which is 2×3

$2 + 3 + 4 = 9$, which is 3×3

$3 + 4 + 5 = 12$, which is 4×3

$(n - 1) + (n) + (n + 1)$

$n - 1 + n + n + 1 = 3n$

Yes, this is true for all integers.

> First, try it out with some more sets of three consecutive integers. You could work systematically.
>
> Once you are convinced that it works, try to think about why.
>
> There are several different ways of explaining this. To start with, think about a general set of three consecutive numbers.
>
> Using algebra you can simplify this expression.
>
> The expression simplifies to $3n$ ($3 \times$ the middle number). So it must be true for all integers.

b $n + (n + 1) + (n + 2) + (n + 3) = 4n + 6$

> You could do this algebraically, where n is the first number.

c

Number of numbers	Rule based on the first number being n
2	$2n + 1$
3	$3n + 3$
4	$4n + 6$
5	$5n + 10$
6	$6n + 15$
7	$7n + 21$
8	$8n + 28$

> The method for part **b** can be extended for any number of numbers.

10   **a** $430 \div 142 = 3.028\,169...$

        $400 \div 142 = 2.816\,901...$

        $250 \div 142 = 1.760\,563...$

        $430 \div 125 = 3.44$

        $400 \div 125 = 3.2$

        $250 \div 125 = 2$

        $430 \div 10 = 43$

        $400 \div 10 = 40$

        $250 \div 10 = 25$

        She can fit $3 \times 2 \times 40$ CD cases into the packing box.

        240 CDs will fit into each box.

> Start by considering the different ways in which the CDs could be arranged. Check whether 142 mm will divide into 43 cm, 40 cm, 25 cm.

> Check whether 125 mm will divide into 43 cm, 40 cm, 25 cm.

> Check whether 10 mm will divide into 43 cm, 40 cm, 25 cm.

> The answers in bold give the smallest error while using all the dimensions of the box and the CD.
>
> Look for best fits.
>
> $430 \div 142 = 3.028169...$
>
> $250 \div 125 = 2$
>
> $400 \div 10 = 40$

   b   Three boxes will hold all 600 CDs, so she will need two more boxes.

---

11   **a**   Translations of $\begin{pmatrix} 0 \\ a \end{pmatrix}$

        Where a is any number: positive, negative or zero.

> Daisy's shape can move up or down. This means the x-coordinate stays the same but the y-coordinate can vary.

   b   Translation of $\begin{pmatrix} b \\ b \end{pmatrix}$

        Where b is any number: positive, negative or zero.

> For the shape to stay on the line $y = x$, it must move up and right by the same amount.

12 **a** 1 Try a different starting shape.

    2 Try a different pair of perpendicular mirror lines.

    3 Try a different starting position for the shape.

Mikey has looked at one example and drawn his conclusion based on this.

b

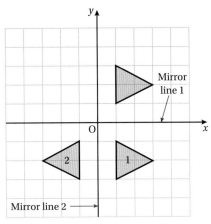

If you carry out the reflection in Mikey's chosen mirror lines ($y = 0$ and $x = 0$) with this new shape it becomes clear that something else is happening: the shape has been rotated 180° about the origin.

Because Mikey's original shape was a rectangle, it has rotational symmetry and he therefore did not notice that the rotation had happened.

His conclusion was not incorrect, but it was not the full answer. That depends on the nature of the starting shape.

---

13 The perimeter of the large semi circle is

$$\pi \times \frac{6}{2} = 9.42\ldots \text{ cm}$$

Treat the perimeter as a large semi circle and a smaller circle.

Now find the diameter of the smaller circle.

This is the hypotenuse of a right-angled triangle.

$d^2 = 2^2 + 3^2$

$d = \sqrt{13} = 3.605\,55\ldots \text{ cm}$

Circumference $= \pi \times 3.606\,55\ldots \text{ cm} = 11.327\ldots \text{ cm}$

Total perimeter $= 9.42\ldots + 11.327\ldots = 20.7 \text{ cm (3 sf)}$

---

1 Estimating the areas, handprint A is approximately 5 times larger than handprint B.

Method 1: Count the squares that are more than half inside the large handprint. Do the same for the small handprint. Divide the area of handprint A by the area of handprint B to find how many times bigger it is.

Method 2: Count the whole squares inside the large handprint. Match up the part squares, to see how many whole squares you can make. Find the total. Do the same for the small handprint. Divide the area of handprint A by the area of handprint B to find how many times bigger it is.

> This is a question about area. The following are two methods you could use to estimate the area.

2 **a** 1.099 and 1.308 – both start with 1.

1.099 and 1.308 – in the tenths position 3 is bigger than 0, so 1.308 is bigger than 1.099.

b 0.5 is equal to 0.50 and 0.500, so 0.5 = 0.500

c 1.7 and 1.534 – both start with 1.

1.7 and 1.534 – in the tenths position 7 is bigger than 5, so 1.7 is bigger than 1.534.

> Use your knowledge of place value in this question.

3 $2x - 1 + 2x - 1 + x + 3 = 41$

$5x + 1 = 41$

This gives $x = 8$, so the sides are 11 cm, 15 cm, 15 cm.

> Write an equation for the perimeter of the triangle and then solve it.

> You can check your answer by confirming that these lengths add up to 41.

4 **a** $\dfrac{4}{30} = \dfrac{2}{15}$

b $4 \times 5 = 20$

c $\dfrac{2}{15}$

> 4 yellow balls and 30 balls in total

> This is the same as the answer to part **a**. A ball chosen at random (to be first or to be furthest), has a probability of $\dfrac{2}{15}$ of being yellow.

5　**a**　Ratio of water : sugar solution : lemon juice

2500 : 500 : 750

250 : 50 : 75

10 : 2 : 3

b　2500 + 500 + 750 = 3750

= 3.75 litres

c　10 : 1 : 3

d　2500 + 250 + 750 = 3500

= 3.5 litres

> Simplify the ratios to the simplest form.

> Here you need to convert the quantities so that they are all in the same units.

> Start with the ratio in part **a** and then halve the sugar solution.

 6

Husband		Son
8	57	
9 8 5	58	1 7 8 9 9
5 5	59	1 3 3 4
6 1	60	2 4
3 1	61	
3	62	

Key: 57 | 4 = 57.4 g

This shows that there are more packets that are less than 60 g than are 60 g or more, so the farmer is wrong to label the packets 60 g.

The median is 59.5 g for her husband and 59.1 g for her son.

It might be better to label the packets as being 59 g instead.

> A stem-and-leaf diagram would be a good way to display the data.

137

a The smallest the population could be is 6.5 billion.

> In this question, rounding, upper and lower bounds are needed.

> The number 7 has been obtained by rounding to the nearest whole number (of billions).

> This means that the actual number could have been rounded up to 7. For example, 6.9 would round up to 7, and so would 6.6. In fact as long as the number was 6.5 or greater then it would round up to 7.

b The largest the population could be is just less than 7.5 billion. (7.5 billion would round up to 8 billion.) 7.5 billion is the upper bound.

c The population, p, is greater than or equal to 6.5 billion and is less than 7.5 billion.

Where p is the population of the Earth:

$$6\,500\,000\,000 \leq p < 7\,500\,000\,000$$

d If it has been rounded to the nearest billion then it can vary by 999 999 999.

---

8 It might be sensible to assume a working day of 8 hours (9 am – 5 pm).

> Clearly this is a joke, but assume it is accurate. You need to make some assumptions about Nick's 'normal' working hours.

a A full working day would be 8 × 60 minutes = 480 minutes. 5% of this is 24 minutes, so Nick would work 24 minutes on a Friday.

> Calculate the amount of time spent working on Friday. 5% of 8 hours is 0.4 of an hour. This doesn't mean very much, so let's change the 8 hours into minutes.

b On Wednesday Nick would work 40% of 480 mins (192 mins). On Monday he would work 12% of 480 mins (57 mins and 36 seconds). Therefore, subtracting, Nick would work 134 mins and 24 seconds (2 hours 14 mins 24 seconds) more on a Wednesday.

c It might look as if it must be Nick because he works for 23% compared to Bernard's 18%, but if Bernard's working hours are longer then 18% of a larger amount could be bigger than 23% of something smaller.

9

a $t + 15$

This is similar to other questions involving writing expressions and equations.

Let t be the cost of a jam doughnut in pence. The iced doughnut is 15 more than this.

b $3t + 5(t + 15) = 1195$

$3t + 5t + 75 = 1195$

$8t = 1195 - 75$

$8t = 1120$

$t = 1120 \div 8 = 140$

Cost of jam doughnut is £1.40, cost of iced doughnut is £1.55

If you get six of each then it will cost

£1.40 × 6 + £1.55 × 6

= £17.70

10   **a** 225 minutes = 3 hours 45 minutes

A lot of information in the question is irrelevant. The carving time is the same for both birds. The turkey weighs 4.5 kg more, so it needs to be in the oven for 50 minutes × 4.5 longer.

b $t = 50m + 30$

Convert the time to minutes then substitute in the equation from part **b**.

c $5 \times 60 + 5 = 305$ minutes

$(305 - 30) \div 50 = 5.5\,\text{kg}$

d 9.25 am if no carving time is required.

9.05 am if 20 minutes of carving time is needed.

11 a $\frac{2}{11}$

2 letter Ts in MATHEMATICS: 11 letters in total

b $\frac{2}{11} \times \frac{1}{10} = \frac{1}{55}$

If first card is T (probability $\frac{2}{11}$) there is one T left out of 10 cards.

12 a $320 = k(8 \times 10)$

This is a question about proportionality.

$320 = 80k$

$k = 320 \div 80 = 4$, so each square metre costs £4

The area of the lawn = $12 \times 8 = 96 \, \text{m}^2$

cost = 4 × area

Cost = constant of proportionality × area

$\qquad$ = 4 × 96 = £384

b Area = 560 ÷ 4 = 140 m²

The lawn could have any dimensions that multiply to give 140:

14 m × 10 m

7 m × 20 m

5 m × 28 m

13 a Her children get $\frac{1}{2} + \frac{1}{3} = \frac{3}{6} + \frac{2}{6} = \frac{5}{6}$

So the pets get $1 - \frac{5}{6} = \frac{1}{6}$

b 3 : 1 : 1 : 1

Use the fractions to split up the whole into sixths.

c Each daughter: $\frac{1}{6} \times £5\,000\,000 = £833\,000$

d $\frac{3}{5}$ remains, which is £3 million

The children each get $\frac{1}{4} \times £3$ million = £750 000

This is similar to the problems you have already solved in this question.

e The remaining $\frac{1}{4}$ is shared between five grandchildren: £750 000 ÷ 5 = £150 000

f £2 500 000 : £750 000

10 : 3

14 a i   turkey : chicken = 4 : 7 = 1 : 1.75

Multiply by 6 to get   6 : 10.5

10.5 kg of chicken is needed

ii 250 g of herbs needed for 4 kg turkey

125 g needed for 2 kg turkey

250 + 125 = 375 g of herbs needed

b   turkey : chicken

4 : 7

16 : 28

16 kg of turkey

c   herbs : turkey : chicken

250 : 4000 : 7000

1 : 16 : 28

Simplifying ratios is a useful idea here.

Multiply ratio by 4.

Change all quantities to grams.

Divide by 250.

15

This involves similar ideas to the previous question.

a 4800 Chelsea supporters

21 parts = 25 200 supporters

1 part = 25 200 divided by 21 = 1200

The number of Chelsea supporters = 1200 × 4

b 6000 children

4 adults : 1 child

One fifth of total attendance are children

Total = 25 200 + 4800 = 30 000

$\frac{1}{5}$ of 30 000 are children

c 18 000 more adults

30 000 – 6000 = 24 000 adults

24 000 – 6000 = 18 000 (adults – children)

d 2000 ice creams

$\frac{1}{3}$ of the children have ice creams

6000 ÷ 3

e 36 000 soft drinks

24 000 adults

Half of adults have 3 soft drinks each

12 000 × 3

f ice cream : soft drinks

2000 : 36 000

1 : 18

16 **a** 10 km

> Use the travel graph to help you answer the questions.

b 20 minutes. The speed is slow because driving in a large city, Edinburgh.

c 2 stops, for a total of 20 minutes

d First stage of the return journey from 20:30 to 20:40.

> The graph is steepest at this point.

e 30 km in 10 minutes means 180 km/h

f 20:55

g 38 km

h 90 km ÷ 3 h = 30 km/h

i 90 km/h

17

> It is useful to recognise that a travel graph is likely to help here.

> To help you to draw Pauline's graph you know that she goes 6 km in each hour.
>
> Emma's mum rides at 24 km/h. 16 km is $\frac{2}{3}$ of 24 km, so it takes her 40 minutes to cycle the 16 km.

a 10:10

b 6 km

c 12 km

d 12:10

e 6 km/h

f 5 km

18 $a^2 + b^2 = c^2$

$32.3^2 + 57.7^2 = 4372.58$

but $80^2 = 6400$

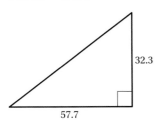

Jenny must have measured the diagonal incorrectly because Pythagoras' theorem doesn't work with her measurements. She has over-estimated the diagonal length (which is actually 66.1 cm).

> This is a Pythagoras question.

19 **a** Price = $k \div$ mileage

$2000 = k \div 10\,000$

$k = 20\,000\,000$

Price = $20\,000\,000 \div$ mileage

b £1000

c 5000 miles

> Use k as the constant of proportionality in an inverse proportion formula.

20 **a**

Height = 18 inches

Aspect ratio = 32 : 18

This simplifies to 16 : 9

> In order to calculate the aspect ratio you need to know the height of Carlos's TV.
>
> You know the diagonal length and the width so you need to apply Pythagoras' theorem.

b

$(9x)^2 + (16x)^2 = 42^2 = 1764$

$337x^2 = 1764$

$x^2 = 1764 \div 337$

$x = \sqrt{1764 \div 337} = 2.287...$ inches

Width = $16x = 16 \times 2.287... = 36.6$ inches (to 1 dp)

Height = $9x = 9 \times 2.287... = 20.6$ inches (to 1 dp)

> The aspect ratio of the TV is 16 : 9 (width : height).
>
> You know the diagonal length so apply Pythagoras' theorem.

> An alternative method would be to work out the scale factor of the enlargement.

1 **a** Idea 1: all the same age group – she should sample people of different ages.

Idea 2: likely to be generally fit anyway as they are involved in sport. Should sample people of different fitness levels. They are also all the same gender – should sample people of both genders.

Idea 3: all the same age range – should sample people of different ages.

b There isn't a time period given (per day, week, month?). 'Sport' isn't defined: does walking the dog (which is exercise) count, or does it have to be competitive?

c There is no box for less than 1 hour. The others overlap – 3 appears in two boxes.

> This is not really maths but is a matter of common sense!

2 Although this is a 3-day weekend, a usual weekend is 2 days so $\frac{1}{2}$ of that needs to be added. It is $\frac{1}{2}$ longer.

> A normal weekend is 2 days, so making it a third longer doesn't seem very easy!

3

> Do a rough estimate first. The garden looks like a rectangle that is roughly 5 m by 12 m. This has an area of roughly 60 m², and at about £2 per square metre the turf would cost about £120 in total.

Width of Nathan's garden = 7 × 80 cm = 560 cm or 5.6 m

5.6 m × 12 m = 67.2 m²

> Area of rectangle 5.6 m wide and 12 m long

1 paving slab = 0.8 m × 0.8 m = 0.64 m²

Area of patio = 15 × 0.64 m² = 9.6 m²

> Area of triangular corner missing from top left

Area = $\frac{1}{2}$ × 0.6 m × 1.5 m = 0.45 m²

Area of turf = 67.2 m² – 9.6 m² – 0.45 m² = 57.15 m²

The turf will cost 57.15 × £2.34 = £133.73

4 The exact area is $550 \times 90 + 270 \times 60 = 65\,700\,m^2$

An acre is about $68 \times 105 \div 2 = 3570\,m^2$

The field is about $65\,700 \div 3570 = 18.4$ acres

$18.4 \times 2 = 36.8$

Do a rough estimate first. The field is roughly the same as this rectangle:

550 m

120 m

550 m is about $5 \times 105\,m$ and 120 m is about $2 \times 68\,m$, so 10 football pitches will fit. This is about 20 acres, so 40 cows could be kept on the land.

So Rebecca could keep about 37 cows on this land.

This is close to the initial estimate of 40.

5 B is the best estimate (even though D is closest to the actual answer).

A common way to estimate an answer is to round off the numbers in the question to 1 sf.

This would give $50 \times 20 \div 10 = 100$.

6 Kristie runs 10 miles each day, which is 16 km. Kristie is training a little more than Amar, but we don't know anything about the lengths of time they have been training, how generally fit they are, how old they are, whether they are doing other fitness work etc. so we can't really tell who is better prepared.

You can do some calculations but should also think about what is sensible.

7 **a** In the original recipe there is $150\,g + 120\,g = 270\,g$ of dark chocolate.

$270\,g \times 2.5 = 675\,g$

You need to convert a recipe for 8 people to a recipe that serves 20 people.

You could divide by 8 to find the ingredients for one serving and then multiply by 20.

Alternatively, you could multiply by $\frac{20}{8}$, which is the same as multiplying by $2\frac{1}{2}$.

b 4 bars of 200 g each (because 3 bars is only 600 g)

c $800\,g - 675\,g = 125\,g$

675 : 125

27 : 5

d $\frac{3}{4}$ of 400 g is 300 g

To serve 6 people you can divide by 8 and multiply by 6, or you can multiply by $\frac{6}{8}$. $\frac{6}{8}$ is the same as $\frac{3}{4}$.

8 Let x be the number of birds.

$$\frac{45}{x} = \frac{6}{50}$$

$6x = 45 \times 50$

$6x = 2250$

$x = 375$

There are 375 finches, so the keeper will need to find new homes for 25 of them.

> The fraction of the sample that has rings should be about the same as the fraction of the population that has rings.

9 A pie chart tells you about proportions, not about numbers. It says in the question that all of Year 8 are there, but only a few Year 9s, so even though a large fraction of the Year 9s want to swim, this may not be many people.

> You can deal with this by interpreting the graphs and thinking about what is sensible.

10 The pie chart shows the proportion of the boys' pets that are dogs, cats, etc. We don't know whether one boy owns all the rabbits, for example, or whether there are the same number of boys as there are girls.

This means that we cannot answer the questions from these pie charts.

> As long as you remember that pie charts show proportions this is a question you can answer by thinking about what is sensible.

11 a Coach Cooksey will have the more accurate mean height as he is using the actual height of each of his players. Coach McKay is finding the estimated mean using the midpoints of each class interval. By using the midpoints he is giving each player in each class interval the same height.

Team McKay			
Height (cm)	**Midpoint**	**Frequency**	**Midpoint × frequency**
$145 \leqslant h < 155$	150	1	150
$155 \leqslant h < 165$	160	2	320
$165 \leqslant h < 175$	170	2	340
$175 \leqslant h < 185$	180	8	1440
$185 \leqslant h < 195$	190	3	570
$195 \leqslant h < 225$	210	4	840
Totals:		20	3660

b $3660 \div 20 = 183$ cm

c The mean height is the same for both teams at 183 cm.

But Team Cooksey has both the shortest player = height 142 cm and the tallest player = height 226 cm, so that team has a larger range of heights.

12 **a** $(x - 6) \times (x - 1)$

$= x^2 - 7x + 6$

So Vanessa is correct.

> Area involves multiplying, so it is likely that x^2 will be involved, so Vanessa's expression looks more plausible. To work out the area of a rectangle we do length × width.

b Perimeter $= 4x - 14 = 2(2x - 7)$

> Perimeter is the distance around the outside of the shape.
>
> This can be factorised to give $2(2x - 7)$, which is Doug's expression.

 13 $\sqrt{81} = 9$

> Start by working out each one.

$4^2 - 2^3 = 16 - 8 = 8$

$\sqrt[3]{1000} = 10$

$5\sqrt{25} \div 9^0 = 5 \times 5 \div 1 = 25 \div 1 = 25$

$3^{-2} \times 3^2 = 3^0 = 1$

$(\sqrt{36})^2 = 6^2 = 36$

1, 8, 9, 10, 25, 36

> Now put the values in order from smallest to largest.

$3^{-2} \times 3^2, 4^2 - 2^3, \sqrt{81}, \sqrt[3]{1000}, 5\sqrt{25} \div 9^0, (\sqrt{36})^2$

> Finally write the numbers in order in their original formats.

 14 **a** $2328 \, \text{km/h}$

> $1455 \div 5 \times 8$

b $1746 \div 2328 = 0.75 \, \text{hour} = 45 \, \text{minutes}$

> Time = distance ÷ speed

c $9700 \div 2328 = 4\frac{1}{6} \, \text{hours} = 4 \, \text{hours and } 10 \, \text{minutes}$

> ($\frac{1}{6}$ hour = 10 minutes)

d Take-off, accelerating up to speed, decelerating and landing are all at much lower speeds. There might also be strong winds and other bad weather.

a 1500 m ÷ 200 m = 7.5

Simon will need to run 7.5 laps of the indoor running track and 3.75 laps of the outdoor running track to cover 1500 m.

Given that the other track is twice as long, he will need half as many laps.

b 5 km = 5000 m

5000 m ÷ 200 m = 25

Denise will have to run 25 laps of the indoor track and 12.5 laps of the outdoor track to cover 5 km.

The 10 km is double the 5 km race, so Denise will have to run 50 laps of the indoor track and 25 laps of the outdoor track to cover 10 km.

 a $t = 40k + 25$, where k is the number of kilograms.

b No, he will need to put it in the oven at 9.25 am.

$40 \times 3.75 + 25$ plus an extra 10 minutes of time is 185 minutes. This is the same as 3 hours and 5 minutes.

 a

		Day 1		
		Swim	**Jog**	**Cycle**
Day 2	**Swim**	SS	JS	CS
	Jog	SJ	JJ	CJ
	Cycle	SC	JC	CC

This is one way to list all the possibilities in a systematic way.

b $\frac{1}{9}$

c $\frac{6}{9}$

$= \frac{2}{3}$

All of the combinations except SS, JJ and CC.

This is sensible because whichever one is chosen for Day 1, there are 2 out of the 3 that can be chosen on Day 2.

18 **a** Glass 1 contains $\frac{1}{4}$ units of squash.

Glass 2 contains $\frac{1}{6}$ units of squash.

Pouring the two glasses together results in a total volume of 2 units.

The squash from glass 1 now represents $\frac{1}{8}$ of the combined drink.

The squash from glass 2 now represents $\frac{1}{12}$ of the combined drink.

$$\frac{1}{8} + \frac{1}{12} = \frac{3}{24} + \frac{2}{24} = \frac{5}{24}$$

So the resulting drink is $\frac{5}{24}$ squash.

b The strength of the final drink will be between the two strengths of the original drinks. $\frac{2}{5}$ and $\frac{3}{10}$ are both less than $\frac{1}{2}$ so it is not possible to make a drink that is exactly $\frac{1}{2}$ apple.

> With questions like this it can help to assign a volume to the glass, be it a numerical value or an algebraic one.
>
> Assume the volume of each glass is 1 unit so that you can just work with the fraction in the question.

> Notice that this will produce a drink that is weaker than glass 1 and stronger than glass 2.

---

19 **a** 10% of 90 g = 9 g

5% of $90\,\text{g} = \frac{9\,\text{g}}{2} = 4.5\,\text{g}$

The low-fat yogurt contains more sugar per pot (5.9 g compared to 4.5 g for the 'full-fat' version).

b $5.9\,\text{g} \div 90\,\text{g} = 0.06555...$

$0.06555... \times 100\% = 6.555...\%$

$\frac{4.5\,\text{g}}{90\,\text{g}} = 5\%$

The low-fat yogurt contains approximately 6.6% of the GDA of sugar.

The full-fat yogurt contains 5% of the GDA of sugar.

> Calculate the amount of sugar in grams in the second yogurt.

> Conclusion.

> First consider the low-fat yogurt.

> Next consider the full-fat yogurt.

> Conclusion.

20 **a**

Planet	Distance from the Sun in AU	Shortest distance to next orbit in AU
Mercury	0.387	0.336
Venus	0.723	0.277
Earth	1	0.524
Mars	1.524	3.679
Jupiter	5.203	4.32
Saturn	9.523	9.685
Uranus	19.208	10.879
Neptune	30.087	–

The distance between Venus and Earth is the smallest, at 0.277 AU.

b $0.277 \times 9.3 \times 10^7 = 25\,761\,000$ miles
(or 2.5761×10^7 miles)

Earth is never closer than 25 million miles to Venus.

The planets are not always the same distance apart. If Earth and Mars are on the same side of the Sun then they will be closer than if they are on opposite sides. That is why the question asks for the 'shortest possible distance'.

 21

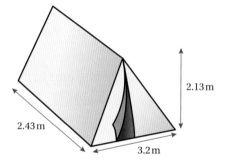

2.13 m

2.43 m

3.2 m

Peter is 2.03 m tall so the tent needs to be at least this long. You might assume that to be comfortable Peter will need the tent to be a little longer, for example an extra 20 cm at his head and at his feet.

To decide how wide the tent needs to be you have to make an assumption about the 'width' of Peter and his three friends. You want it to be comfortable so you should be generous with your estimate. Perhaps allowing 80 cm per person is reasonable.

Peter also needs to be able to stand up in the tent. If the tent is 2.03 m tall then Peter would just about be able to stand up in the middle (but his head would touch the top). So again, make it more comfortable and give him a little extra room, say 10 cm.

1 Candice should give the mean length.

> The mode = 11 cm
>
> The median = 10.25 cm
>
> The mean = 9.833 cm

2 $\frac{1}{3}$ of 12 = 4 purple sections

$\frac{1}{6}$ of 12 = 2 red sections

$\frac{1}{12}$ of 12 = 1 green section

$4 + 2 + 1 = 7$

$12 - 7 = 5$ blue sections

> You could use the diagram from the question and colour it in.

3 **i, ii** The only numbers that can be on the dice are 1, 2, 3 and 4.

> Each piece of information tells you something useful.

  iii There is only one 1.

  iv Six of the numbers are 2 or 4.

  v Three of the numbers are 1 or 4.

  The numbers are: 1, 2, 2, 2, 2, 3, 4, 4

  Five of these are prime numbers, so the probability of getting a prime is $\frac{5}{8}$.

> **iii** tells you there is only one 1, so **v** tells you there are two 4s. **iv** then means there are four 2s, so the other number must be a 3.

4 **a** $\frac{1}{6}$

  b $\frac{1}{6} \times 12 = 2$

  The expected number of sixes in 12 throws is 2. However, this is the expected average number over many sets of 12 throws, so Bashir is not completely correct.

> Probability of an event × total number of outcomes = expected number of favourable outcomes

5 **a** $(17 \times 3) - 14 = 37$ runs

b It depends. Here is a table showing the number of runs Ben might score and the number that John would get:

Ben	0	1	2	3	4	5	6	7	8	9	10	11	12	13
John	–14	–11	–8	–5	–2	1	4	7	10	13	16	19	22	25

After this John's score will increase faster than Ben's.

If Ben usually scores less than 7 then he is better, but if he usually scores more than 7 then John is better.

c If Ben scores 4 runs or fewer then John would have a negative number of runs, which is not possible.

6 **a**

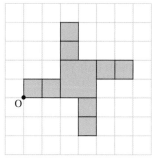

b 0 lines of symmetry

c Rotational symmetry order 4

d 1 Draw a circle of radius 1 cm.

 2 Enlarge this circle by a scale factor of 2 about the centre of the circle.

 3 Translate the small circle 2 cm to the left.

 4 Translate the small central circle 2 cm to the right.

There are several ways this image could be created. Here is one possible set of instructions.

a, b

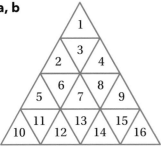

There are 16 small triangles.

1, 2, 3, 4

2, 5, 6, 7

4, 7, 8, 9

5, 10, 11, 12

7, 12, 13, 14

9, 14, 15, 16

6, 7, 8, 13

So there are 7 equilateral triangles of this size.

1, 2, 3, 4, 5, 6, 7, 8, 9

2, 5, 6, 7, 10, 11, 12, 13, 14

4, 7, 8, 9, 12, 13, 14, 15, 16

So there are 3 equilateral triangles of this size.

16 small + 7 medium + 3 large + 1 extra large = 27 similar triangles

> All equilateral triangles are similar because they all have three equal angles (of 60°).

> Triangles 1, 2, 3 and 4 make another equilateral triangle. Count all the equilateral triangles of this size.

> Triangles 1, 2, 3, 4, 5, 6, 7, 8 and 9 make a larger equilateral triangle. Count all of these.

> Finally there is a single extra large equilateral triangle made from all 16 smaller triangles.

 A

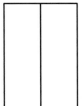

> This is likely to be a triangular prism.
> A sketch might help:

B

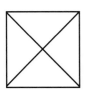

> A sketch suggests a pyramid.

C

> A sketch suggests another triangular prism.

9　**a** $\frac{2}{3}$ as a decimal is 0.666... so $\frac{2}{3} > 0.66$

It is much easier to compare them if they are both fractions or are both decimals.

b $0.25 = \frac{1}{4}$

$\frac{8}{32} = \frac{1}{4}$, so $0.25 = \frac{8}{32}$

In this pair, the fraction can actually be simplified. This will make the comparison easier.

c $\frac{3}{11} = 0.272727...$

so $\frac{3}{11} < 0.273$

Use short division to evaluate the decimal equivalent to $\frac{3}{11}$.

In this question it is easier to compare the decimals (finding a common denominator to compare the fractions is not as easy).

d $0.05 = \frac{5}{100} = \frac{1}{20}$,

$\frac{1}{20} > \frac{1}{22}$, so $0.05 > \frac{1}{22}$

e Here is a diagram showing 0.49

Now if you shade 0.4999 of the shape you get this (there is a tiny part of that top square which hasn't been shaded):

If you keep on doing this you get closer and closer to 0.5 each time, so we say that 0.4999 ... = 0.5

10 **a** Jillian's polygon is a regular pentagon.

> It has 5 sides. 5 is a prime number.
>
> It has rotational symmetry of order 5.
>
> All the interior angles are obtuse (greater than 90° but less than 180°).

b 'I am a quadrilateral.' This could describe any four-sided shape.

'I have two pairs of parallel sides.' The following quadrilaterals match this description: square, rectangle, parallelogram, rhombus.

c To get the answer 'square', she could add: 'the angles are all 90° and the sides are all the same length'.

If she adds: 'the sides are all the same length' then the shape will be a rhombus, but it could also be a square (because squares are also rhombuses).

If she adds 'angles are all 90° then the shape will be a rectangle, but it could also be a square (because all squares are rectangles).

All of these are already parallelograms, so she doesn't need to add anything.

11 **a** Equilateral triangle

> You know that the angles in an equilateral triangle are all 60°.

b i Square

> You know that all the angles in a square are 90°.

ii Regular hexagon

> The exterior angle = 180° – 120° = 60°
>
> The sum of exterior angles is 360° for all polygons.
>
> 360° ÷ n = 60° (where n is the number of sides of the polygon).
>
> $n = 6$

iii Regular decagon

> Similarly to shape **ii**, the exterior angle is 180° – 144° = 36°
>
> 360° ÷ 36° gives 10 sides.

12 a 9 cm²

> The area of the letter H can be found very easily by counting squares.

b One way to split Y is:

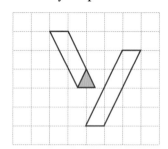

> The letter Y can be split into the shapes shown in the diagram.
>
> An alternative is to assemble parts to make whole squares.

Area of right-hand parallelogram = 1 cm × 4 cm = 4 cm²

> Area of a parallelogram = base × perpendicular height

Area of left-hand piece
= (1 cm × 3 cm) − (0.5 × 1 cm × 1 cm)
= 3 cm² − 0.5 cm² = 2.5 cm²
4 cm² + 2.5 cm² = 6.5 cm²

> Area of left-hand piece = area of parallelogram − area of shaded triangle

> Total area of Y.

c The letters B and D both fit inside a rectangle of area 12cm².

> For part **c** you don't actually need to work out the areas of the two letters.

To make the B you need to subtract 1 square. To make the D you need to subtract more than 1 square, so the B has a bigger area.

d The smallest area will be the letter I. This is because all other shapes have an I shape as part of their construction (and then have additional pieces added).

 13

Pattern number	1	2	3	4
Number of metal rods	6	12	18	24
Number of wooden rods	7	12	17	22

> You could draw a few more diagrams and could then make a table of results to see whether that will help you see what is going on (although it won't explain it).

a 18

> The number of metal rods goes up by 6 each time because each new panel has 6 metal rods in it.

b 22

> The number of wooden rods goes up by 5 each time because when a new panel is added, the left-hand side is joined to the previous panel.

c 6n

d The 6 × 12 = 72 metal rods will cost £144, and the 5 × 12 + 2 = 62 wooden rods will cost £155.

The total cost is £299.

14 Shape A, the circle, could be the circular face of the cylinder (the cross-sectional area), the base of a cone or any view of a sphere.

Shape B, the square, could be any face of a cube, a square face of a cuboid or the curved surface of a cylinder.

All three boys were correct.

To answer this question you need to think about each boy's answer in turn and decide if there is a face on the 3-D shape they have named that matches the plan view given in the question.

 15

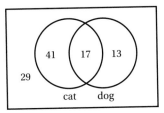

A Venn diagram will help to show what is going on.

Fill the 17 in first.

Then use the information about how many people own a dog.

Then use the information about how many people own either a dog or a cat but not both.

Finally, fill in the ones who own neither a dog nor a cat.

a $\frac{29}{100}$

b $\frac{41}{100}$

16 **a** The blue graph is MoveIt Builders.

b MoveIt Builders = £15

Read the information from the graph.

c £14

£70 for 5 days, daily rate = £70 ÷ 5

d Less. It is £12 daily, so £2 less per day.

MoveIt Builders £75 for 5 days (£75 – £15 = £60, £60 ÷ 5)

e £75

f £183

£15 + (£12 × 14)

g MoveIt Builders

JCEs would charge £ 14 × 14 = £196

h £13 cheaper

17 **a**

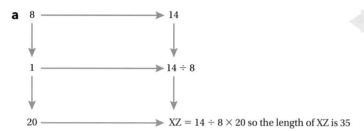

XZ = 35 cm

b Triangle ABC has area 80 cm².

Triangle XYZ has area 245 cm².

c The ratio is 80 : 245, which simplifies to 16 : 49.

d 16 and 49 are both square numbers.

The ratio of the sides is 4 : 7.

The ratio of the areas is $4^2 : 7^2$.

Draw a proportion diagram to work out y.

18

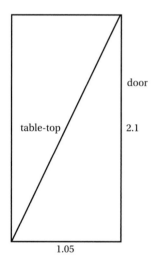

The table-top diameter is 240 cm = 2.4 metres, which is more than the height of the door. To check whether it will fit when tilted at an angle, work out the length of the diagonal of the doorway.

$a^2 + b^2 = c^2$

$2.1^2 + 1.05^2 = c^2$

$5.5125 = c^2$

$c = \sqrt{5.5125} = 2.347... \, \text{m}$

Arthur's new table has a diameter of 240 cm. Even if Arthur turns the table to try to go through the door diagonally, it will not fit: it is more than 5 cm too big.

19

a 80% of £10 is £1 × 8 = £8.

75% of £12 is $\frac{3}{4}$ of £12 = £9.

75% of £12 is more money.

b One way is to work out that 20% of one hour is 12 minutes, whereas $\frac{3}{8}$ of half an hour is $11\frac{1}{4}$ minutes.

An alternative is to compare 20% with $\frac{3}{8}$ of a half. $\frac{3}{8} \times \frac{1}{2} = \frac{3}{16}$ but 20% = $\frac{1}{5} = \frac{3}{15}$, so 20% is bigger.

c 50% of 1 is $\frac{1}{2}$. 25% of 2 is also $\frac{1}{2}$. They are the same.

d A 10% discount would be £1.299, which is less than the £1.99 postage charge, so a 5% discount is not enough and it would be cheaper to buy it in the shop.

There are lots of ways of carrying out these comparisons. Some of them are shown here.

You don't need to do any difficult calculations.

20

Write the lengths as ordinary numbers.

a Rectangle B has the bigger perimeter.

Perimeter of A is 16 + 9 + 16 + 9 = 50

Perimeter of B is 25 + 2 + 25 + 2 = 54

b Rectangle A has the bigger area.

Area of A is 16 × 9 = 144

Area of B is 25 × 2 = 50

21 **a** $4x + 5y = 205$ (equation 1)

$3x + 7y = 235$ (equation 2)

Let x be the price of each apple in pence, and y be the price of each banana in pence.

b, c

One way to solve this is to get the same number of xs in each equation.

$12x + 28y = 940$

Multiply equation 2 by 4

$12x + 15y = 615$

Multiply equation 1 by 3

$13y = 325$

Subtract

$y = 25$

Divide by 13

This means a banana costs 25 pence.

$4x + 5 \times 25 = 205$

Substitute $y = 35$ into equation 1.

$4x = 80$

$x = 20$

so an apple costs 20 pence.

 22 **a**

Altogether all four rectangles add up to $20x - 36$

b $20x - 36 = 204$

$20x = 240$

$x = 12$

This means $3x$ is 36 and $(2x - 5)$ is 19.

The dimensions are 36 cm by 19 cm.

This is one way to split up the shape.

The top rectangle has area: $2(3x - 4) = 6x - 8$

The left rectangle has area: $2(2x - 5) = 4x - 10$

a $1\,m^3 = 1\,m \times 1\,m \times 1\,m$

$1\,m^3 = 100\,cm \times 100\,cm \times 100\,cm$

$1\,m^3 = 1\,000\,000\,cm^3$

Anna was incorrect to think that she should multiply by 100. She should have multiplied by 1 000 000.

b $0.15 \times 1\,000\,000 = 150\,000\,cm^3$

c $150\,000\,ml \div 1000 = 150$ litres $(1\,cm^3 = 1\,ml)$

150 litres = 150 one-litre bottles of cola

Alternatively, you could spot that Anna is wrong by thinking about how small $15\,cm^3$ is. $15\,cm^3$ is the volume of a cuboid that is $1\,cm \times 1\,cm \times 15\,cm$ (the height of your ruler).

This wouldn't be very much water to have a bath in!

 a There are two possibilities:

Rotate A 180° about (0, 3).

Enlarge A by a scale factor of –1 about point (0, 3).

b There are a lot of possibilities:

Do two reflections (e.g. in the line $x = 0$ and then in the line $y = 3$).

Do a rotation and a translation (e.g. rotate A 180° about (–2, 3) and then translate it 4 units to the right.

Do a translation and then a rotation, or two enlargements, or an enlargement and a translation.

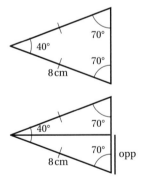

Triangle B is isosceles and is congruent to triangle A.

Triangle C doesn't have any lengths marked on it, so while it is similar to A and B you don't know that it is congruent.

Triangle D is not congruent to the others because the third side is 5.5 cm instead of 5.4723... cm

A and B are definitely congruent, so statement **e** is correct.

If you use the fact that triangle A is isosceles you can work out the other angles.

Splitting an isosceles triangle in half gives two right-angled triangles, so in triangle A:

$Opp = 8 \times \sin 20° = 2.736\,16...\,cm$

The length of the third side is twice this length.

$2 \times 2.736\,16... = 5.4723...\,cm$

1 **a**

+	1	2	3	4	5	6	7	8	9
1									
2									
3									
4									
5									
6									
7									
8									
9									

Systematically pair up every integer with every other integer.

The table illustrates all the possible calculations that can be made.

Notice that these are different calculations. They do not necessarily represent different answers.

The answer is 45.

b

	−9	−8	−7	−6	−5	−4	−3	−2	−1
−9	−18	−17	−16	−15	−14	−13	−12	−11	−10
−8	−17	−16	−15	−14	−13	−12	−11	−10	−9
−7	−16	−15	−14	−13	−12	−11	−10	−9	−8
−6	−15	−14	−13	−12	−11	−10	−9	−8	−7
−5	−14	−13	−12	−11	−10	−9	−8	−7	−6
−4	−13	−12	−11	−10	−9	−8	−7	−6	−5
−3	−12	−11	−10	−9	−8	−7	−6	−5	−4
−2	−11	−10	−9	−8	−7	−6	−5	−4	−3
−1	−10	−9	−8	−7	−6	−5	−4	−3	−2

The shaded cells show the 17 different answers you can get.

2

1 – can't do

2 – can't do

3 = 3

4 – can't do

5 = 5

6 = 3 + 3

7 – can't do

8 = 3 + 5

9 = 3 + 3 + 3

10 = 5 + 5

11 = 3 + 5 + 3

12 = 3 + 3 + 3 + 3

7 is the largest number you cannot make.

This is an obvious one to work through systematically.

Now you might notice that you can make 11 by adding 3 onto the way you made 8. To make 12 you can add 3 onto 9, to make 13 you can add 3 onto 10. This means you can always make every number bigger than 7 by adding on extra 3s.

7 is the largest number you cannot make.

3

1 – only has 1 factor	7 – prime	13 – prime
2 – prime	8 – factors are 1, 2, 4, 8	14 – factors are 1, 2, 7, 14
3 – prime	9 – factors are 1, 3, 9	15 – factors are 1, 3, 5, 15
4 – factors are 1, 2, 4	10 – factors are 1, 2, 5, 10	16 – factors are 1, 2, 4, 8, 16
5 – prime	11 – prime	17 – prime
6 – factors are 1, 2, 3, 6	12 – factors are 1, 2, 3, 4, 6, 12	(needs to be smaller than 18)

The number 12 has the most factors.

You could work through this systematically, working out the number of factors that each number has. You can save yourself some time by recalling that prime numbers have exactly two factors, so you can eliminate them immediately.

4 **a** 16 × 130 mm = 2080 mm = 208 cm

16 edges of hexagons make up the perimeter.

b The perimeter is 156 cm and each side is 13 cm

156 ÷ 13 cm = 12

This can be done with three interlocking hexagons, each showing four edges.

12 edges need to be 'exposed'.

You could try 2 hexagons and see that this won't give you enough sides (there are only 10), and then try 3 hexagons in a line and find there are 14 sides, so there must be a different collection of 3 hexagons that will work.

5 **a**

Number of flowers	1	2	3
Number of blue beads	6	12	18

18 blue beads are needed.

b Each flower needs 6 blue beads so the nth term is $6n$.

6 **a** 30

We are using relative frequency, so if you double the throws, you need to double the number of sixes.

b $7 \times 50 = 350$

105 sixes are seven times as many as 15 sixes, so you need seven times as many throws.

c $0.3 \times 1200 = 360$

Part **a** tells you the relative frequency is $\frac{30}{100} = 0.3$

7 **a** $10 \times 7 = 70$

$11 \times 6 = 66$

$10 \times 7 > 11 \times 6$

You could work out answers to all the multiplications and compare them, but there are quicker ways for some of them.

b $-44 \times 5 = 44 \times -5$

You don't need to work out that both of them equal -220. They contain the same numbers and one of them is positive and one is negative each time. This means that the answers are the same.

c $972\,310 \times 0 < 1 \times 1$

While it is easy to work out the answers to this one you don't need to, because you know that anything multiplied by zero is zero, and the second answer is positive.

d $91 \times -2 < 59 \times 3$

The first answer is negative (because there is a positive number multiplied by a negative number), whereas the second answer is positive (because there are two positive numbers multiplied together). This means you don't need to work out the exact answers (-182 and 117).

8 $+ - \times$: $5 + 2 - 10 \times -3 = 5 + 2 - -30 = 5 + 2 + 30 = 37$

$+ \times -$: $5 + 2 \times 10 - -3 = 5 + 20 + 3 = 28$

$- + \times$: $5 - 2 + 10 \times -3 = 5 - 2 - 30 = -27$

$- \times +$: $5 - 2 \times 10 + -3 = 5 - 20 - 3 = -18$

$\times + -$: $5 \times 2 + 10 - -3 = 10 + 10 + 3 = 23$

$\times - +$: $5 \times 2 - 10 + -3 = 10 - 10 - 3 = -3$

You can achieve a negative result in three different ways.

Make a systematic list of the arrangements of the three operations and then calculate the answers.

9 **i** $100 \div (5^2 \times 2)$

$100 \div (25 \times 2)$

$100 \div 50 = 2$

> The only sensible way to answer this question seems to be to work out each answer. Remember the correct order of operations (where, for example, brackets are worked out first).

ii $620 \times 4 \div 248$

$2480 \div 248 = 10$

iii $81 - 37 \times 2$

$81 - 74 = 7$

> Using the correct order of operations, multiplication comes before subtraction. 37×2 must be done first.

iv $-27 \div -3 + 12$

$9 + 12 = 21$

Calculation **i** is the smallest.

---

10 **a** **i** $2 \times 3 \times 4 = 24$

> Gemma appears to be multiplying the numbers.

ii Gemma is not correct, as 12 is the smallest integer that is divisible by 2, 3 and 4.

iii Lidia's method:

It can't be smaller than 6 because those numbers didn't work for both 2 and 3.

It can't be 6 because 4 won't work.

It can't be 7 because none of the numbers will work.

It can't be 8 because 3 won't work.

It can't be 9 because 2 and 4 won't work.

It can't be 10 because 3 and 4 won't work.

It can't be 11 because none of the numbers work.

It can be 12 because 12 is divisible by 2, 3 and 4. The answer is 12.

> Lidia's method is to work systematically, checking each number.
>
> This will get her the correct answer. However, it takes a long time.

Harry's method:

2, 4, 6, 8, 10, 12, 14, 16, 18, 20, ...

3, 6, 9, 12, 15, 18, 21, 24, 27, ...

4, 8, 12, ...

12 is in all three lists. The answer is 12.

> Harry's method is to write out the times tables and look for common multiples.
>
> His method is good: it gets him the correct answer and is quicker than Lidia's method in this case.
>
> However, if the question was about different numbers that have times tables that aren't as quick to write down, or that don't have common multiples very early on in the lists, Harry's method would take much longer.

iv You are trying to work out the Lowest Common Multiple of 2, 3 and 4. $2 \times 2 \times 3$ will do this, giving an answer of 12.

b 30 is the smallest number exactly divisible by 3, 5 and 6.

Whichever method you use you should get 30 as the answer.

12 **a i**

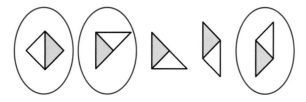

With two sandwiches it is possible to create three different polygons: a right-angled isosceles triangle, a parallelogram and a square.

If you have two sandwiches (two triangles) then it might make sense to keep one of them fixed and move the other around it. Here the blue one is fixed and the white one moves.

There are five different positions in which the second sandwich could be placed, three of which make different polygons.

ii

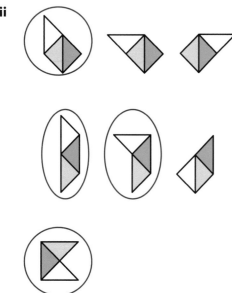

If you have three sandwiches (three triangles) then it makes sense to start with the three arrangements for two sandwiches and move the third sandwich around these.

The second and third shapes that start with a square are congruent to the first one – and the others that start with a square will also all be congruent or reflections.

The third shape is congruent to the ones above. All the others that start with the parallelogram will be congruent to others that we already have.

This is the only new shape formed by starting with the right-angled isosceles triangle.

With three sandwiches it is possible to create four different polygons: two different trapeziums and two different irregular pentagons.

Conclusion.

iii

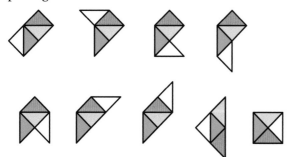

If you have four sandwiches (four triangles) then it makes sense to start with the four arrangements for three sandwiches and move the fourth sandwich around these.

Again, some of these are identical or are reflections of each other.

These are the ones that are distinct.

With four sandwiches it is possible to create nine different polygons: a rectangle, an irregular pentagon, three different irregular hexagons, an isosceles trapezium, a parallelogram, an isosceles triangle and a square.

b Yes.

This is almost a trick question. A square is an example of all the special quadrilaterals (it is also a rectangle, a parallelogram, a rhombus, a kite and a trapezium), so the original sandwich works for all of them.

a Box 1: four cylinders of radius 10 cm and height 15 cm

Box 2: one cylinder of radius 20 cm and height 15 cm

Box 3: sixteen cylinders of radius 5 cm and height 15 cm

c Box 1: vol. of cylinders = $\pi \times 10^2 \times 15 \times 4 = 6000\pi$

Box 2: vol. of cylinder = $\pi \times 20^2 \times 15 = 6000\pi$

Box 3: vol. of cylinders = $\pi \times 5^2 \times 15 \times 16 = 6000\pi$

Because the total volume of the cylinders is the same each time, the unused space is the same in each box.

Did this answer surprise you? Or did you guess that all three boxes had the same amount of unused space?

If you look at each calculation for the volume of the cylinders, you will notice that each has $\pi \times 15$. The rest of the calculation for each volume multiplies to give the same answer, 400.

$4 \times 10^2 = 20^2 = 16 \times 5^2 = 400$

 a

	Crisps	**Fruit**	**Yogurt**
Water	sandwich, crisps, water	sandwich, fruit, water	sandwich, yogurt, water
Juice	sandwich, crisps, juice	sandwich, fruit, juice	sandwich, yogurt, juice

Every meal includes a sandwich, so you only need to consider crisps/fruit/yogurt and water/juice. A table is a good way to show this.

b $\dfrac{2}{6} = \dfrac{1}{3}$

Two combinations out of six that include yogurt

c $\dfrac{2}{6} \times 330 = 110$

Two combinations out of six that include crisps

167

15

a $\frac{24}{48} = \frac{1}{2}$

b $\frac{1}{2}$

c $\frac{9}{48} = \frac{3}{16}$

d $\frac{1}{48}$

e $\frac{9}{48} = \frac{3}{16}$

> Be careful: the question says the number is greater than 1 and less than 50 so it can only be from 2 to 49.

> There are 48 numbers and 24 of them are even.

> All the other numbers are odd.

> There are 9 multiples of 5.

> The factors of 48 that are between 1 and 50 are: 2, 3, 4, 6, 8, 12, 16, 24 and 48.

16 $12 \times 50\,\text{p} = £6$ (12 coins)

$9 \times £1 = £9$ (9 coins)

$£47 - £6 - £9 = £32$, which is 16 £2 coins

$12 + 9 + 16 = 37$ coins in total

Probability that a £2 coin is shaken out $= \frac{16}{37}$

> First work out how many £2 coins there are.

> To work this out we need to assume that each coin is equally likely to appear when the money box is shaken.

17 **a**

	Circle	Star	Triangle
Heart	CH	SH	TH
Rabbit	CR	SR	TR
Car	CC	SC	TC

> This is one way to list all the possibilities in a systematic way.

b $\frac{1}{9}$

18 **a** $\frac{3}{12} = \frac{1}{4}$

b $\frac{3}{12} \times \frac{2}{11} = \frac{6}{132}$

$\frac{1}{22}$

> 3 blue pens and $8 + 1 + 3 = 12$ pens in total

> If the first pen was blue, there are two blue pens left among the remaining 11 pens.
>
> Multiply the probability of the two independent events.

> Simplify.

19 **a** 12 panels ÷ 4 = 3 panels on each side

3 × 60 cm = 180 cm

A diagram will help with this question.

The area is 180 cm × 180 cm = 32 400 cm^2

b

Let the number of panels along the shorter side be a.

From the number of panels available:

$12 = 2a + a + 2a + a = 6a$

$a = 12 ÷ 6 = 2$

The run is 4 panels long and 2 panels wide.

This area is 240 cm × 120 cm = 28 800 cm^2

Adam is not correct. This pen has a smaller area than the square pen.

c 12 panels ÷ 3 = 4 panels per side.

4 × 60 cm = 240 cm

Area of a triangle = 0.5 × base × height (h)

Use Pythagoras' theorem to work out the height of the triangle.

$h^2 = 240^2 - 120^2$

$h^2 = 43\,200$

$h = 206.846...$ cm

Area = $\frac{1}{2}$ × 240 cm × 207.846... cm

= 24 941.53... cm^2, which is smaller than the square pen, so Kim is wrong.

20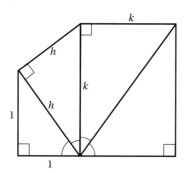

This problem can be solved using some of the strategies from earlier chapters. First label the diagram. You could also put on the things you know.

a All the triangles are similar, so they must all be isosceles.

$$1^2 + 1^2 = h^2$$

$$2 = h^2$$

$$h^2 + h^2 = k^2$$

$$2 + 2 = k^2$$

$$k = 2$$

Focus on the first triangle on the left and use Pythagoras' theorem.

Now focus on the next triangle. You don't need to square root the 2 and then square it again.

The fourth triangle is the same as the third one, so the width is 2 and the height is 2.

The area of the first triangle is $\frac{1}{2}$ and the area of the largest one is 2, so the area has been multiplied by 4.

b The triangles are all isosceles and have a right angle, so the other two angles must be 45° each. The four angles that are marked are all 45°, which adds up to 180° so it does form a straight line.

21 All powers of 1 are 1, so this means that $2^b + 3^c = 244$.

The powers of 2 and 3 won't be negative because negative powers would give fractions.

This question can be worked out in several different systematic ways. Here is one.

3^c is always odd, so the only way to get an even result (like 244) is for 2^b to be odd. But any power of 2 greater than 0 is an even number, so b must be 0.

You could make a list of powers of 2 and powers of 3, but this is a quicker method.

So $2^0 = 1$ and $3^c = 243$

3^0	1
3^1	3
3^2	9
3^3	27
3^4	81
3^5	243

This means that:

a can be anything

$b = 0$

$c = 5$

1 **a** In Dallas, each room costs $75 for one person plus $35 per extra person and each room has three beds.

> There is a lot of information here! Pick out the pieces that you need for the question.

In one room, it will cost $75 for the first person, $35 for the second person and $35 for the third person. That makes $145 in total for each room for three people.

There are 15 people altogether, so they need five rooms and overall this will cost:

$145 × 5 = $725

b In Las Vegas, the motel has rooms with four beds, so they will need three full rooms and one with three people in it.

> A diagram might help.

Room 1: ($75)($35)($35)($35) 4 people, cost = $180

Room 2: ($75)($35)($35)($35) 4 people, cost = $180

Room 3: ($75)($35)($35)($35) 4 people, cost = $180

Room 4: ($75)($35)($35) 3 people, cost = $145

Total cost is $685.

$725 – $685 = $40

It is $40 cheaper to stay in Las Vegas.

c

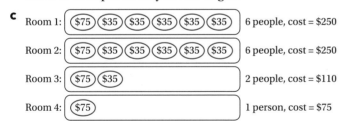

Room 1: ($75)($35)($35)($35)($35)($35) 6 people, cost = $250

Room 2: ($75)($35)($35)($35)($35)($35) 6 people, cost = $250

Room 3: ($75)($35) 2 people, cost = $110

Room 4: ($75) 1 person, cost = $75

> The question doesn't tell you to work out how much it will cost in San Francisco, but you will need to if you want to know which city is cheapest.

The total cost is $685, so Las Vegas and San Francisco are equally cheapest at $685.

2 **a**

The total length is 1400 m. Three laps will be:

1400 m × 3 = 4200 m, which is 4.2 km

Use the diagram in the question but try to complete the missing labels.

Once all the sides are labelled, you could add them to find the length of one lap.

Alternatively, you could use the fact that the length of the track is the same as the perimeter of the rectangle around the edge.

b The runners have run 7 laps in total.

1400 m × 7 = 9800 m, which is 9.8 km

3 There are 12 inches in 1 foot, so 5 feet 10 inches is:

5 × 12 + 10 = 70 inches

You know that Sarah is 5 feet 10 inches tall and that 1 inch is approximately 2.5 cm. Maybe the best thing to start with is to convert her height into inches.

70 inches = 70 × 2.5 cm = 175 cm

This means that Leon is 5 cm taller than Sarah, so he is correct.

4 He will have $3 left.

$3 ÷ 1.70 = £1.76

There are two ways to do this. Here is one:

5 **a** Jyoti's tower = 1 + 2 + 3 + 4 + 5 + 6 = 21 cm

Indira's tower = 7 + 8 + 9 + 10 + 11 + 12 = 57 cm

Indira's tower is 36 cm taller.

One way to do this is to write out the heights of the two towers.

b 57 + 21 = 78 cm

One possible answer is 1 + 2 + 3 + 10 + 11 + 12 = 39 and 4 + 5 + 6 + 7 + 8 + 9 = 39

The total height of all the cubes is 78 cm.

78 ÷ 2 = 39 cm gives the height of each tower when they are the same. Each girl must have a combination that is 39 cm high.

6 There are eight numbers: _ _ _ _ _ _ _ _

The biggest number is 16: _ _ _ _ _ _ _ 16

What does each piece of information tell you?

Start putting the numbers in order.

The mean is 7.5. This tells you that they all add up to
$8 \times 7.5 = 60$

The range is 15. This means that the biggest minus the
smallest is 15, so the smallest is 1.

1 _ _ _ _ _ _ 16

The mode is 3 and 5. This tells you that there must
be more 3s and 5s than everything else and the same
number of 3s and 5s. There might be two of each or
three of each. If there are two of each you have:

1 3 3 5 5 _ _ 16

The total so far is 33, which means the other two
numbers must add up to 27 (because the mean tells
you they all add up to 60). The other two numbers
can't be another 3 and a 5 (because they only add up
to 8).

The bigger of the two remaining numbers must be at
most 15 (because if it was 16 then the mode would be
16 too). If the bigger number is 15, then the remaining
number must be 12.

If the bigger of the two numbers is 14 then the other
one is 13.

The numbers could be either of these two sets:

1 3 3 5 5 12 15 16

1 3 3 5 5 13 14 16

7 **i** True

If you add the digits of the number together you
get 48, which is divisible by 3, so the number is
also divisible by 3.

ii False

The number is a multiple of 3, so it cannot be
prime. It is also even.

iii True

The number 12 345 678 910 is in the 5 times table,
so if you divide 12 345 678 912 by 5 then the
remainder is 2.

iv True

The last two digits are 12, which is a multiple of 4,
so the number is a multiple of 4. Tip: if a number
is a multiple of 4 then the last two digits will also
be a multiple of 4.

8 Grandad's age is $2x$, Geoff's age is x and Paul's age is $x - 28$.

One way to do this is to call Geoff's age x and to work out the other ages in terms of x.

In total this is $2x + x + x - 28$, which equals 112.

$4x - 28 = 112$, so $4x = 140$ and $x = 35$.

9 **a** $c = 17 \times 55 + 60$

$c = 995$

The advert costs £9.95.

b $2100 = 17n + 60$

$n = 120$

c A 55-word advert costs £9.95 and the formula tells you that if you increase the number of words by 1 then the cost will increase by 17 pence. This means that 55 words is the most Jolene can get for £10.

You know the answer to part **c** already, because part **a** has given it away.

10 $\pi \times 4^2 \times 15 = 753.98 \, \text{cm}^3$ (2 dp)

Start by working out the volume of water.

Volume of water bottle (cylinder) = area of circular base × height

15

4

$753.98 \, \text{cm}^3 = 753.98 \, \text{ml}$

Volume of water in bottle (in ml).

$753.98 \, \text{ml} \div 100 \, \text{ml} \times 2 = 15$ scoops

11 **a** $1:8$

Ratio of teachers to students

$x:140$

Let number of teachers = x

$x = 140 \div 8 = 17.5$

Number of teachers must be a whole number

18 teachers

b $21 \times 8 = 168$

Every adult can have 8 students to supervise

$168 - 140$

A total of 168 students can go

28 more students

c The ratio of students to teachers is:

$140:21$

$= 20:3$

12 **a**

original shape

b

original shape

c

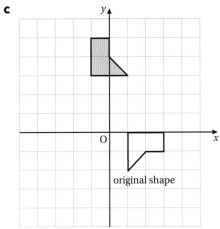

original shape

Tracing paper can help with rotations.

0.74 or $\dfrac{74}{100}$	0.46 or $\dfrac{46}{100} = \dfrac{23}{50}$	0.9 or $\dfrac{90}{100} = \dfrac{9}{10}$
0.86 or $\dfrac{129}{150} = \dfrac{43}{50} = \dfrac{86}{100}$	0.7 or $\dfrac{70}{100} = \dfrac{7}{10}$	0.54 or $\dfrac{54}{100} = \dfrac{27}{50}$
0.5 or $\dfrac{50}{100} = \dfrac{1}{2}$	0.94 or $\dfrac{94}{100} = \dfrac{47}{50}$	0.66 or $\dfrac{33}{50} = \dfrac{66}{100}$

Remember that in a magic square all the rows and columns and both main diagonals add up to the Magic Number. The key idea here is to convert everything into the same type of number. It is easiest to work in either decimals or fractions with a denominator of 100. The diagram shows possible answers: you only need one answer in each square.

 1 pint (imperial) is 0.568 litres (568 ml).

9 pints = 568 ml × 9 = 5112 ml

We know there are two different units in the question: millilitres and pints.

Convert pints into millilitres.

5112 ml = approximately 5000 ml

$= 5 \times 10^3$ ml of blood in James's body.

The question asks you to work with approximate figures.

There are 5×10^9 red blood cells per millilitre of blood, so in total James has about

$5 \times 10^9 \times 5 \times 10^3$

$= 25 \times 10^{12} = 2.5 \times 10^{13}$ red blood cells

10% of $2.5 \times 10^{13} = 0.25 \times 10^{13}$

The number of remaining blood cells is $2.5 \times 10^{13} - 0.25 \times 10^{13} = 2.25 \times 10^{13}$

15 　**a** Volume of planter box = 100 cm × 80 cm × 70 cm

$\qquad\qquad\qquad\qquad\quad$ = 560 000 cm³

Work in cm because you need to know the volume in cm³.

560 000 cm³ = 560 000 ml

Volume of planter box (in litres).

560 000 ml = 560 litres

560 litres ÷ 50 litres = 11.2

So she will need 12 bags of compost to fill the planter box.

Number of bags of compost required. You can't round down as you would normally do because 11 bags won't be enough.

b 12 ÷ 3 = 4

How many times can Flo use the special offer?

4 × £12 = £48

Cost of 12 bags of compost, using the special offer.

c 12 × £5.99 = £71.88

Cost of 12 bags of compost at the regular price.

£71.88 – £48 = £23.88

Savings when she uses the special offer.

16 　**a** Probability of 8 kits in a litter = 1 − (0.1 + 0.2 + 0.3 + 0.3)

The probabilities should add up to 1.

$\qquad\qquad\qquad\qquad\qquad\qquad\qquad$ = 0.1

A table might help.

+	4	5	6	7	8
4			10		
5		10			
6	10				
7					
8					16

b 0.1 × 0.1 = 0.01

c P(4 kits and 6 kits) = 0.1 × 0.3 = 0.03

P(5 kits and 5 kits) = 0.2 × 0.2 = 0.04

P(6 kits and 4 kits) = 0.3 × 0.1 = 0.03

Any of these outcomes are possible, so add them together to get

(0.3 × 0.1) + (0.2 × 0.2) + (0.1 × 0.3) = 0.2

17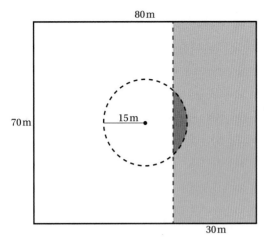

The dark-pink shaded area shows the part the goat can eat.

You could draw a rectangle measuring 8 cm by 7 cm.

The goat is tethered on a rope measuring 15 m.

On this diagram, the locus of points within which the goat will be is a circle of radius 1.5 cm with the centre in the middle of the field.

Measure 3 cm from the end of the field to show where the wheat is planted.

18

A clear, well-labelled diagram will be useful. This one focuses on the important triangle.

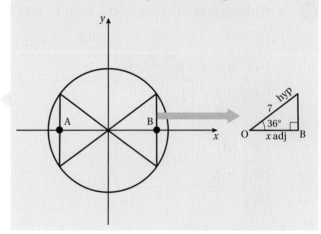

OB = cos 36° × 7 cm = 5.663... cm

To work out x you need to use trigonometry.

B: (5.66, 0)

Now interpret this in terms of the coordinates of point B (values rounded to 2 dp).

A: (−5.66, 0)

Point A is a reflection of point B in the y-axis.